A Wasting Historical Asset?

A Comparative Study of Grave Memorials at
Wootton Wawen, King's Norton and
Birmingham, C. 1700-1940

Iola A. Shorters

BAR British Series 366
2004

Published in 2019 by
BAR Publishing, Oxford

BAR British Series 366

A Wasting Historical Asset?

ISBN 9781841713625 paperback
ISBN 9781407320083 e-book

DOI https://doi.org/10.30861/9781841713625

A catalogue record for this book is available from the British Library

This book is available at www.barpublishing.com

BAR Publishing is the trading name of British Archaeological Reports (Oxford)
Ltd. British Archaeological Reports was first incorporated in 1974 to publish
the BAR Series, International and British. In 1992 Hadrian Books Ltd became
part of the BAR group. This volume was originally published by John and
Erica Hedges in conjunction with British Archaeological Reports (Oxford) Ltd /
Hadrian Books Ltd, the Series principal publisher, in 2004. This present volume
is published by BAR Publishing, 2019.

BAR
PUBLISHING

BAR titles are available from:

       BAR Publishing
       122 Banbury Rd, Oxford, OX2 7BP, UK
EMAIL   info@barpublishing.com
PHONE +44 (0)1865 310431
  FAX   +44 (0)1865 316916
       www.barpublishing.com

CONTENTS

List of Figures

iii

Acknowledgements

This book is essentially the thesis written under the supervision of Dr. S.R. Bassett of the School of History in the University of Birmingham and accepted for the degree of Master of Philosophy in 2003. Many thanks to Dr. Bassett for his unfailing patience, advice, help and support in the preparation of this thesis.

I would also like to thank several members of the Department of Modern History for their advice and support and also Dr Peter Jupp, Dr Julian Litten, Joseph McKenna and Reverend Dr John Sharp, for taking time to assist me in my research.

A few changes have been made since the thesis was written, in the light of suggestions made by the examiners of the thesis. Responsibility for any errors rests with me.

I gratefully acknowledge the assistance and support of the clergy and ministers of both Wootton Wawen and King's Norton and I would also like to thank them both for allowing me to work freely in the churchyards.

I would like to thank all of my family and friends for their support and interest, particularly Andrew for solving computer problems and Ann for helping me to solve various last minute crises. Finally, a special thank you to my parents, who have always encouraged us in all of our endeavours.

Iola Shorters
March 2004

Abbreviations

When recording the grave memorials each stone was given an individual record number. When an individual grave memorial is referred to throughout the publication it will be cited using this number. For example, memorial record number 1, which is situated in section A of the churchyard, will be referred to as MA1. Memorials from inside the church will be referred to as MCH for memorials in the chancel, MN for the nave, MSA for the south aisle, MNA for the north aisle, MSC for the south chapel.

Introduction

This study was a detailed comparative analysis of the grave memorials in the churchyard of King's Norton (an area of Birmingham which has become increasingly urban in recent centuries), of those in the yard at Wootton Wawen (a deeply rural part of Warwickshire), and of those surviving in several churchyards and two municipal cemeteries in Birmingham, all of which served an area which was wholly urban in character for the entire period of study. The ultimate historical objective was to examine whether important aspects of local communities in significantly different socio-economic environments were reflected in the memorials. The second main objective of the study was to discover the extent to which a well preserved graveyard is, both in isolation and in combination with other sources, a reliable and representative database for local history. How informative and reliable are grave memorials, individually and in groups, as a source of historical evidence? Could grave memorials be used to throw important light on the history of a community if there were no other appropriate records available? Are grave memorials in any respect a unique historical source containing evidence that cannot be obtained from elsewhere?

The first aim of the research was to produce a detailed individual record of the extant grave memorials. All entries in the burial registers for the same periods were studied and the data gathered from these was collated and analysed to investigate a number of demographic, socio-economic, iconographical and other trends. These include trends in life expectancy and in time of death within the year; trends in family composition and typical marriage patterns; changing attitudes to death and disposal of the dead; the graveyards' growth over time, examined by spatial analysis; and, most importantly, the possibility of increasing divergence between the trends at King's Norton and at Wootton Wawen which can be interpreted in terms of increasing rural urban differentiation.

Grave memorials are a primary source of evidence which, in comparison to written sources, has been given hardly any attention at all. Are grave memorials undervalued as a source and can they provide interesting and original results on demography, socio-economic trends and attitudes to death? The question is worth researching because although there has been much written work about funeral customs, there has been little on grave memorials. A number of studies have indicated the potential wealth of information that can be found from memorials but there is still much work to be done in this field considering that churchyards are constantly under threat from clearance and destruction. Even without these threats memorials are a decaying body of historical evidence. Irreplaceable evidence disappears year by year because the memorials are subject to natural decay,[1] such that their lifespan is estimated at approximately 200 to 250 years[2] unless they are carefully preserved. The threat of natural decay combined with regular clearance of

graveyards has pushed written work to concentrate on the need for showing the importance of recording and preserving grave memorials. There have been several excellent works showing how to record graveyards,[3] but most of the written work concentrates almost exclusively on the iconography of the memorials, which is seen as the most powerful argument for their preservation since it and the accompanying epitaphs not only are aesthetically appealing but also provide information about attitudes to death which cannot be obtained from elsewhere. The most comprehensive work on the subject remains *English Churchyard Memorials*,[4] written in 1963. This provides a wealth of information about types of memorials, symbolism, imagery, ornament, lettering, inscriptions and epitaphs, and memorial manufacture. The emphasis on iconography has meant that other forms of historical data from grave memorials have often been overlooked. It is disappointing that in recent years more detailed work has not been done on the usefulness of memorials for local history, demography, genealogical studies and religious attitudes. Several people have discussed how memorials could be used to investigate these trends, but they have stopped short of analysing what can be done with the data once it is collected. There are few comprehensive studies of a single yard and it appears that no systematic comparative study has ever been undertaken. Hopefully this research will help to demonstrate what can be achieved when using grave memorials as a historical source.

The study focuses on the grave memorials of St Nicholas's, King's Norton and St Peter's, Wootton Wawen. Originally in Worcestershire, the large parish of King's Norton included the now separate ecclesiastical parishes of King's Norton, Moseley, King's Heath and Wythall.[5] It became increasingly urban in the nineteenth and twentieth centuries, as it became ever more influenced by the rapidly industrialising and expanding town of Birmingham. As a result the trade and population of the parish increased enormously throughout the nineteenth century, the most populous areas being Moseley and King's Heath which were the closest to Birmingham.[6] Ever more people who were connected with the trade and manufacturing of the town began to live in the suburbs. The people of King's Norton became even more closely connected to Birmingham when tram facilities and suburban railways developed in the 1870s,[7] and it was included administratively in the city of Birmingham under the Birmingham Extension Act of 1911.[8]

St Nicholas's churchyard is also a good choice as it is a large and fairly well preserved yard. Recording will be made easier because extensions to the churchyard in the twentieth century mean that nearly all of the more modern stones lie separate from the memorials which will be used for this study. It was decided to record the memorials at both churchyards from the earliest datable stones until 1940. This means that the study does not include more modern memorials which are often still visited by relatives and friends.

The other churchyard to be used for the comparative analysis is at St Peter's, Wootton Wawen. Until recently Wootton Wawen was in an extremely rural part of Warwickshire. The parish of Wootton Wawen included the small village of Wootton Wawen, the hamlet of Ullenhall and the small borough of Henley-in-Arden.[9] The population of Henley-in-Arden fell after the mid-nineteenth century, probably as a result of its industries being moved to larger industrial centres.[10] The parish was brought closer to Birmingham and Stratford-upon-Avon by the main road and railway links which developed in the late nineteenth and early twentieth centuries, but the area remained rural and preserved its 'wild and wooded' character.[11] Again Wootton Wawen's churchyard is a good choice as it is fairly well preserved. The extension made in 1927 means that the more modern stones lie separate from most of those which have been recorded.

Previously there has been a regional bias in written work on funerary practices and in grave memorial studies towards London, the south-east and urban areas. It will be interesting to compare the results from these two parishes with each other and with similar studies elsewhere. Would the rural parish of Wootton Wawen show similar demographic and socio-economic trends to the increasingly urban King's Norton, and would fashions in first names and trends in iconography, for example, spread more slowly in the more rural area?

Initially it had been intended that the thesis would be a comparative study of these two yards and a third site in the city centre of Birmingham, which was wholly urban in character for the entire period of study. There were restraints on total freedom of choice, however, as many of the city churches have been completely demolished. Even where the churches have survived there has been widespread clearance of their yards. The Birmingham Closed Burial Act, 1878[12] turned 18 yards into public gardens, and since then many more of them have been cleared. Even where some stones have survived, the smaller memorials have often been removed leaving just the large or most ornate monuments behind.

Because there is no suitable site to compare with the other two in full, it was not possible to do a comparative analysis with Wootton Wawen and King's Norton in respect of demographic and socio-economic links, because to do this successfully the third site would need to be a large yard with a good degree of preservation. It was therefore decided to use the remaining memorials in several churchyards and in the two earliest municipal cemeteries in Birmingham and to record only those memorials carrying iconography. These results were analysed so as to discover when the significant changes in iconography occurred and to test the speed at which different symbols became popular. Were the fashions in iconography slower to manifest themselves in Wootton Wawen and King's Norton than in Birmingham?

The study was therefore of memorials from the Roman Catholic church of St Joseph at Nechells,[13] St Margaret's church, Ward End, and the few remaining memorials from St Paul's, Birmingham, and St Philip's, Birmingham. Memorials were also recorded from the General Cemetery, Key Hill and from Warstone Lane cemetery, which were both joint stock cemeteries in Birmingham.[14] The growth of population in the area led to great overcrowding in the churchyards. The Birmingham General Cemetery Company was founded in 1832 and discussion began for a ground for all creeds and denominations.[15] Key Hill Cemetery opened in 1836 and was Birmingham's first public cemetery. In practice the cemetery was used entirely by nonconformists, and so the Church of England Cemetery Company responded to this with Warstone Lane cemetery, which was opened for burials in 1848.[16]

Because the churches at King's Norton and Wootton Wawen are both Anglican it was necessary to consider how large the community of other denominations was in both areas and the date at which non-Anglicans had their own burial grounds. This is an important consideration because there may have been significant non-Anglican influences on the iconography and epitaphs in the churchyards that needed to be taken into account. In the eighteenth century Birmingham and the surrounding area was not a strong centre of Roman Catholicism but the numbers of Roman Catholics increased steadily from 1786, and by the mid-nineteenth century it had become an important centre.[17] Religious dissent was strong and influential in Birmingham.[18] Nonconformism often invaded rural areas where the established church had been dominant.[19] In King's Norton by 1829 there were three Baptist meeting places, one Methodist and one Unitarian chapel.[20] The growth in population in Birmingham and the surrounding area brought much church building by all denominations and religious dissent continued to grow.[21]

Roman Catholicism was the smallest of the major denominations but had strength in rural Warwickshire. The parish of Wootton Wawen was a centre of Catholicism with the support of the Carrington/Smith/Smyth family, who were lords of the manor.[22] Their private chapel at Wootton Hall was used for Roman Catholic masses and services from at least the early seventeenth century until 1905 when the church of Our Lady and St. Benedict was consecrated.[23] As early as 1688 Baptists established themselves in the area but nonconformity was slow to make headway until the nineteenth century. In 1821 in Henley-in-Arden there were 52 recorded dissenters (4.2 per cent of the population of 1249), all of whom were Baptists.[24]

Other places of burial (which will be referred to hereafter as cemeteries) were often a nineteenth century solution to the problems of space and the demands of nonconformists.[25] Before the introduction of cemeteries there is much evidence that other denominations buried their dead in the parish churchyard[26] as independent burial was limited.[27] For Roman Catholics in Wootton Wawen the official Catholic graveyard was opened in 1852. For the inhabitants of King's Norton the only Catholic cemetery in Birmingham was attached to St Joseph's, Nechells, which was opened in 1850. Other

Catholics would have been buried in non-denominational cemeteries.

The other nineteenth century alternative for nonconformists and Roman Catholics was the Burial Law Amendment Act, 1880,[28] which stated that people of all denominations could be buried in Anglican churchyards with the burial conducted according to their own rites. Burials according to this are often indicated in the registers of King's Norton and Wootton Wawen as 'BLAA'. Nonconformists and Roman Catholics are pointed out in the parish registers from 1870 in King's Norton and from 1880 in Wootton Wawen, which shows that even after the introduction of alternative places of burial there were still many people who were buried in the parish churchyard. Before this time it is possible that burials of other denominations were not distinguished in the parish registers from those who were Anglicans although evidence found in studies elsewhere suggests that they may not have been recorded in the parish registers at all.[29]

Not only are the inscriptions on a memorial useful, but the location and its shape and design are too. It was important to record the memorials exactly how they were found, and so for accurate recording it was considered best to use a grave memorial recording form. An appropriately modified version of the form (Figure 1) designed by the Council for British Archaeology was used.[30] As well as a separate recording form for each stone, photographs were taken of memorials where the inscription was difficult to read. Photographs are essential as they often show detail or parts of the inscription that seemed unreadable or highlight words that have been misread.[31] Photographs were also taken of the memorials with iconography on so that they could be used in combination with the drawings of the stones in the analysis of attitudes to death. A careful sketch plan was made of the position of each memorial in the churchyard to show its relative position and to help analyse the topography of the yard. To make recording easier and more accurate, the churchyard at King's Norton was divided up into 12 sections and Wootton Wawen's was divided up into seven sections. A footstone found with a headstone was not recorded separately, but as a component of the headstone on the back of the form. Once all the memorials had been recorded the information was put into electronic databases so as to help collate and analyse it.

There are difficulties when using grave memorials as historical sources. Gravestones are normally not positioned carefully in straight lines, which makes the recording and the drawing of a plan more difficult. There are also problems when trying to record individual memorials. The recording of inscriptions is made difficult and often impossible because some are all but illegible. Grave memorials are exposed to the sun, rain, wind, frost and snow. This can lead to erosion and weathering and can mean that inscriptions have become worn or shallow or have completely disappeared. Air pollution can lead to discolouring of stone, powdering of marble, loss of carved detail and other forms of corrosion of a

monument. Churchyards are often overgrown, with vegetation rendering inscriptions illegible.[32] Ivy erodes the stone, and can virtually cause collapse.[33] Memorials are also subject to fracture from accidental blows, vandalism and frost.[34] Other stones are covered in mud or are found to be sinking, although the inscriptions on these stones are often well preserved. Survival of memorials can be haphazard, related to the quality of the memorial, the care of it, the position of the memorial and whether the space needs to be reused.[35] These problems have been encountered in similar studies. At Wharram Percy[36] recorders had problems because lichens were using the stones as hosts and, more unusually, a wild bees' nest caused concern. At Baswich[37] the main problem was the growths all over the stones; some had just a small amount of ivy on the surface, but others were completely covered. It is also very easy to make mistakes when recording grave memorials. Numbers and words can be misread. It is essential to return to the memorial after the initial recording as things may have been missed, words can look different, or parts of the inscription, which could not be read in a certain light, are now legible.[38]

Few stones survive from before the late eighteenth century, and it is important to consider that this will cause bias in the results. Parish registers are vital when looking at historical demography and for genealogical studies. The grave memorials can be compared to the parish registers to see how reliable the memorials are individually and as a group. The details on individual records can be checked against the parish registers and they can be used in conjunction with the registers to identify family links. Parish registers can also help to fill in missing gaps on individual records because of illegible inscriptions. The reliability of memorials as a group can be tested by comparing the total number of dead people in the yard whom the surviving memorials tell us about, with the actual total number buried there in the same period as recorded in the registers. For example, the reliability of the memorials when investigating age at death and time of year of death can be checked in this way.

There are problems when using parish registers to test how reliable and representative the memorials are and it is important to be aware of the limitations of this written source. The 'accuracy of entries in the parish registers is by no means sacrosanct.'[39] Mistakes have been identified in parish registers throughout the country. In some areas there have been missing or torn out pages, illegible entries and even extensive omissions. Parish registers as source materials are imperfect and the data are not necessarily reliable or complete. Nearly all have odd years missing, some have longer gaps due to the loss of whole books and some have no entries for months because of the death or neglect of the parish clerk.[40] At both King's Norton and Wootton Wawen there were many crossings out and changes of name, and in both parishes the handwriting in some years is almost impossible to decipher.

The people recorded on memorials in Wootton Wawen churchyard were compared to the people in the burial registers to see if they were all listed there. The same was

GRAVE MEMORIAL RECORD SHEET

CHURCH (Parish name/shire) : St Nicholas, King's Norton

1. Date of record:
2. Name of recorder:
3. Memorial record number (and numbers of components):
4. Photograph negative number:
5. Map reference number (location):
6. Type of memorial: a=flat b=head c=tomb
          d= foot e=tablet f=other
7. Material and geology:
8. Stonemason or undertaker:
9. Which faces are inscribed? (N, S, E, W)
10. Number of people commemorated:
11. Period ascription:
12. Condition of monument: 1=sound 2=sound but displaced
          3=leaning 4=fallen 5=damaged
13. Technique of inscription: 1=incised 2=carved in relief
          3=cast in relief 4=lead letters 5=painted
14. Condition of inscription: 1=very good 2=clear but worn
          3=partly legible 4=illegible
15. Dimensions (cms): Height
          Width
          Thickness (headstone)
          Length (tomb)
16. Orientation of grave:
17. Any other distinctive features:
18. Record numbers of memorials of other members of the same family:
19. Parish register check

--INSCRIPTION AND ICONOGRAPHY---

DRAWING/PHOTOGRAPH   INSCRIPTION

Figure 1. Grave memorial recording form

done at Wharram Percy where it was found that where there were discrepancies between the stone and the document, in most cases the document was correct, but in some cases the stone was found to be right.[41] At Wootton Wawen, between 1700 and 1940 15 people who were commemorated could not be found in the parish registers. Some of these died in years where the parish registers were difficult to read, which may explain why they could not be identified, but as the missing people are from years ranging from 1714 to the late nineteenth century, some of those buried in the churchyard are genuinely missing from the registers.

At King's Norton, although the area directly surrounding the church is fairly well preserved, there has been a great deal of clearance in the yard. Many stones were cleared from the north of the church (section J) and 74 memorials were used to form a new pavement in this section (MJ916 to MK988). These are still in relatively good condition, and most of them have been used in full and so are indicated on the plan. Some have also been used in the pavement around the church, and 36 stones or parts of stones have been used to make a boundary wall around section E. All of these have been recorded and, where possible, will be used in all analyses except for discussion of the geography of the graveyard and spatial analysis.

The condition of the stones was relatively good at King's Norton, with only a few being covered by foliage. The worst problems at this site were weathering where often decorative details survive but not the inscription. There were also some memorials that were sinking, and graffiti covered some of the older stones. The worst areas for survival were to the south and east of the church, and ledger stones, chest tombs and some of the pedestal tombs were sometimes totally illegible. The most well preserved inscriptions were often those which were on stones that were leaning forward or had fallen and were now covered by grass or dirt.

One hundred and thirty-nine of the memorials at King's Norton were post-1940, and so although they are shown on the plan, they were not recorded and will not be used in analyses. In total 949 memorials were recorded at King's Norton, 100 of which were illegible and cannot be used in demographical or socio-economic analysis. Many of the illegible stones appear to be of an early date but cannot be deciphered. These were all recorded on the plan. The period ascription was generally taken to be the first date recorded on the memorial, except when the design of the headstone and lettering appeared to conflict with this date. The earliest surviving memorial in the churchyard is dated 1699 (MH641). Considering the date of this memorial, it is surprising that there are only 17 other stones in the churchyard dating from before 1800. The number of memorials recorded increases steadily over the decades presumably as a result of better survival and an increase in population (Figure 2a). In total the memorials at King's Norton contain information about 1644 people. The number of people recorded increases dramatically in

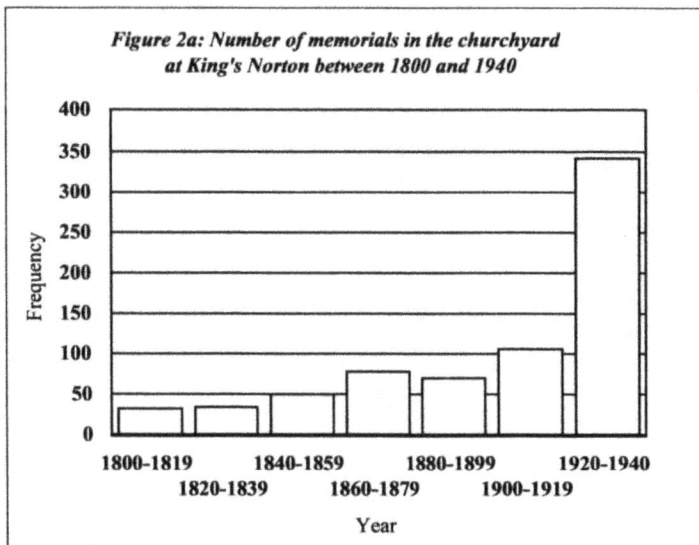

Figure 2a: Number of memorials in the churchyard at King's Norton between 1800 and 1940

the nineteenth and early twentieth centuries and this rise is also shown in the parish registers (Figure 2b).[42] This is undoubtedly due to population growth as ever more people moved outwards from the city centre and lived in residential suburbs like King's Norton. From 1700 to 1799 the memorials at King's Norton represent only 1.14 per cent of people found in the parish registers. Between 1800 and 1899 this increases to 12.5 per cent and even in 1900 to 1940, the memorials represent only 19.5 per cent of the people recorded in the parish registers as having being buried there.

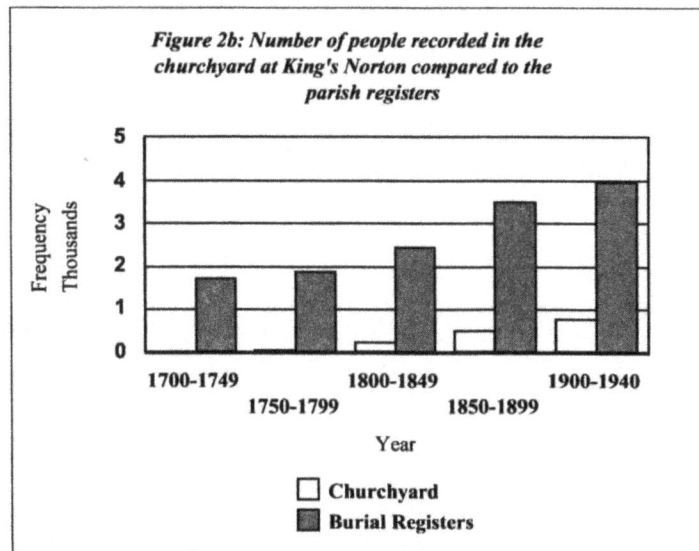

Figure 2b: Number of people recorded in the churchyard at King's Norton compared to the parish registers

☐ Churchyard
■ Burial Registers

The churchyard at Wootton Wawen is fairly well preserved, although a small number of memorials, predominantly footstones, were used to make a stone wall in section EE. These have all been recorded and where possible will be used in all of the analyses except for the discussion of spatial analysis and the geography of the yard.

At Wootton Wawen the condition of the stones was relatively very good, although some of the memorials are covered in ivy, some have sunk or are leaning and a few have fallen over. The worst problem here, however, is weathering. The inscriptions on many of the oldest stones are often partly or totally illegible, and on a few of them only traces of the iconography, which was carved in high relief, remain. The worst areas for survival are to the south and directly north of the church where some of the oldest memorials lie.

One hundred and seventy-two of the memorials at Wootton Wawen were post-1940 and were not recorded or used in analysis but they are, however, included on the plan. In total 438 memorials were recorded at Wootton Wawen. The inscriptions on 32 of these stones were completely illegible. Although the illegible memorials could not be used for looking at demographical and genealogical trends, they could be used when investigating types of memorial found, and their position could be used in spatial analysis of the graveyard. The earliest surviving memorial in the churchyard dates from 1682 (MA29). There is a good survival of pre-nineteenth century stones at Wootton Wawen as there are 35 memorials from before 1800. The number of memorials again increases throughout the nineteenth century (Figure 3a), but falls after 1899. In total the memorials recorded at Wootton Wawen contain information about 611 people. The number of people recorded falls in the twentieth century (Figure 3b). This trend is also found in the parish registers[43] and is possibly a result of the availability of a churchyard at Ullenhall, the increasing use of the yard at St Nicholas's, Beaudesert by Henley people, and the creation of a Roman Catholic yard at Wootton Wawen in 1852. The parish registers were damaged by a flood in the vicarage,[44] which affected the records from 1790 to 1811. It was often just a few entries that were difficult to decipher but for several years whole pages were illegible. The bishop's transcripts[45] were consulted and, where possible, the missing information was filled in from these; however, there were holes in some of the material, and some years were difficult to read, and so there may be a small number of people who have not been accounted for. This could affect the results in the comparison of the people buried in the churchyard with the parish registers (1790 to 1811) and the memorials may be slightly less representative than the results in Figure 3b suggest. From 1700 to 1799 the people recorded on the memorials represent only 1.9 per cent of those recorded in the parish registers. This figure increases to 12.3 per cent between 1800 and 1899. The figures are slightly lower than those found at Baswich,[46] but the records from King's Norton and Wootton Wawen for this period are equally representative. However, between 1900 and 1940, the survival rate at Wootton Wawen is excellent with the people in the memorials representing 32.5 per cent of those in the parish registers. The memorials in both churchyards appear therefore to be a good representative sample of the community of their parishes during the nineteenth and early twentieth centuries.

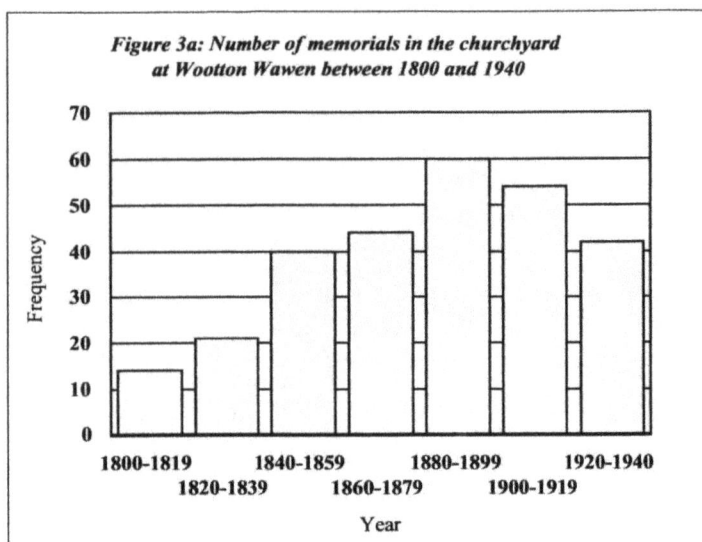

Figure 3a: Number of memorials in the churchyard at Wootton Wawen between 1800 and 1940

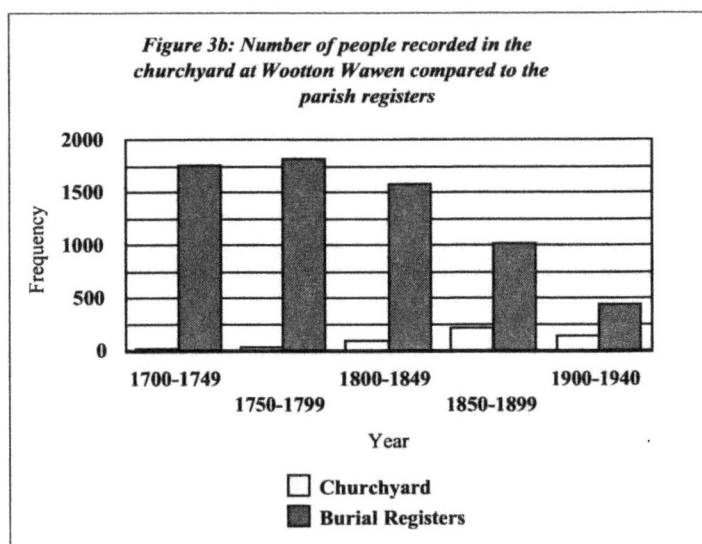

Figure 3b: Number of people recorded in the churchyard at Wootton Wawen compared to the parish registers

[1] W. Rodwell, *The Archaeology of the English Church* (1981), p. 164
[2] W. T. Vincent, *In Search of Gravestones Old and Curious* (1896), pp. 65-66
[3] See H. Mytum, *Recording and Analysing Graveyards* (Council for British Archaeology, 2000) and J. Jones, *How to Record Graveyards* (2nd edn., Council For British Archaeology, 1979)
[4] F. Burgess, *English Churchyard Memorials* (1963)
[5] ed. J. W. Willis-Bund, The Victoria History of the Counties of England, *Worcestershire, Volume III* (1913), p. 179, cited hereafter as VCH, *Worcs*, III
[6] *Ibid.* p. 179
[7] V. Skipp, *The Making of Victorian Birmingham* (1983), p. 180, cited hereafter as Skipp, *Birmingham*
[8] VCH, *Worcs* III, p. 179
[9] ed. L. F. Salzman, The Victoria History of the Counties of England, *Warwickshire, Volume III, Barlichway Hundred* (1945), p. 196, cited hereafter as VCH *Warwick*, III
[10] *Ibid.* p. 209
[11] W. Cooper, *Wootton Wawen: Its History and Records* (1936), p. 3, cited hereafter as Cooper, *Wootton Wawen*
[12] A. Briggs, *History of Birmingham. Volume II: Borough and City, 1865-1938* (1952), p. 114, cited hereafter as Briggs, *Birmingham*
[13] ed. W. B. Stephens, The Victoria History of the Counties of England, *Warwickshire, Volume VII: The City of Birmingham* (1964), p. 408, cited hereafter as VCH, *Warwick*, VII
[14] J. McKenna, *In the Midst of Life: A History of the Burial Grounds of Birmingham* (1992), pp. 11-12, cited hereafter as McKenna, *Burial Grounds*
[15] *Ibid.* p. 12
[16] Chris Upton, *A History of Birmingham* (1993), pp. 139-141
[17] VCH, *Warwick*, VII, p. 399

[18] C. Gill, *History of Birmingham. Volume I. Manor and Borough to 1865* (1952), pp. 77-79

[19] VCH, *Warwick*, VII, p. 420

[20] *Ibid.* p. 419-420

[21] V. Skipp, *Birmingham*, pp. 114-117

[22] ed. W. Page, The Victoria History of the Counties of England, *Warwickshire, Volume II* (1965), pp. 45-46

[23] Cooper, *Wootton Wawen*, p. 88

[24] VCH, *Warwick*, III, p. 209

[25] B. Bailey, *Churchyards of England and Wales* (1987), p. 20

[26] D. E. C. Eversley, 'Exploitation of Anglican Parish Registers by Aggregative Analysis', in ed. E. A. Wrigley, *An Introduction to English Historical Demography: From the Sixteenth to the Nineteenth Century* (1966), pp. 44-96 (p. 50)

[27] J. Rugg, 'The Origins and Progress of Cemetery Establishment in Britain', in eds. P. Jupp and G. Howarth, *The Changing Face of Death: Historical Accounts of Death and Disposal* (1997), p. 111

[28] R. Fletcher, *The Akenham Burial Case* (London, 1974), pp. 268-275

[29] E. A. Wrigley, 'Family Reconstitution', in ed. E. A. Wrigley, *An Introduction to English Historical Demography: From the Sixteenth to the Nineteenth Century* (1966), pp. 96-159 (p. 108), cited hereafter as Wrigley, 'Family Reconstitution'

[30] An example of this is shown in, P. A. Rahtz, 'The Archaeology of the Churchyard', in ed. P. Addyman and R. Morris, *The Archaeological Study of Churches*, Council for British Archaeology Research Report 13 (1976), p. 44

[31] I Shorters, 'A study of the grave memorials of Holy Trinity Church, Baswich, Staffordshire' (University of Birmingham, unpublished BA dissertation, 2000), p. 31, cited hereafter as Shorters, 'Baswich', p. 73

[32] C. Brooks, *Mortal Remains: The History and Present State of the Victorian and Edwardian Cemetery* (1989), p. 111, cited hereafter as Brooks, *Mortal Remains*

[33] H. Lees, *English Churchyard Memorials* (2000), p. 141

[34] Brooks, *Mortal Remains*, p. 111

[35] J. Jones, 'The Grave memorials of the church of St Mary, Deerhurst, Gloucestershire' (University of Birmingham, unpublished BA dissertation, 1972), p. 27

[36] P. Rahtz, 'Wharram Percy memorial stones: an anthropological view from Mars', in ed. D. Hooke, *Medieval Villages* (1985), pp. 214-223 (p. 219), cited hereafter as Rahtz, 'Wharram Percy'

[37] Shorters, 'Baswich', p. 12

[38] *Ibid.* p. 73

[39] H. L. White, 'Monumental Inscriptions', *The Genealogists' Magazine*, 16 (1971), pp. 470-474 (p. 470)

[40] Wrigley, 'Family Reconstitution', pp.106-108

[41] Rahtz, 'Wharram Percy', p. 223

[42] Birmingham Central Library. Registers for burials dating from 1546-1844 are transcribed in, *Registers of the Church of St. Nicholas, King's Norton, Worcestershire. Part three: marriages 1546-1754, burials 1546-1791* (1983) and *Registers of the Church of St. Nicholas, King's Norton, Worcestershire. Part two: baptisms and burial 1792-1844, marriages 1754-1837* (1981). Later registers are on microfilm in the History and Local Studies Department, reference EP4/2/4/2-EP4/2/4/6 for the years 1844 to 1944.

[43] These are held on microfilm at Warwickshire Record Office, DR195/2-DR195/4 for years 1700 to 1812, DR195/13 for 1813-1869, and DR740/3 for 1869-1979.

[44] Cooper, *Wootton Wawen*, pp. 76-79

[45] These are held on microfilm at Worcester Record Office, reference b736, BA 2139/882 to BA 2139/884 for years dating from 1790 to 1792 and reference b736, BA 2015/346-367 for years dating from 1793 to 1811.

[46] Shorters, 'Baswich', p. 12

Chapter One

DEMOGRAPHY

Age at Death

Demographic issues were studied through analysis of the inscriptions on the memorial stones. At King's Norton 1479 people had their age of death recorded on their monument. This meant that 89.9 per cent of the total of 1644 people who were recorded in the churchyard could be included in the investigation of life expectancy. This was slightly higher than at Wootton Wawen where 541 people had their age of death recorded on their monument. This meant that 88.5 per cent of the total of 611 people recorded could be used when looking at life expectancy in this investigation.

Analysis of the total age at death results for King's Norton (Figure 4a) shows that the most frequently recorded age at death is 70-79 (21.5 per cent of the total), followed by 60-69 (18.8 per cent) and 50-59 (13.1 per cent). The least frequently recorded age at death is, unsurprisingly, 100-109 (0.07 per cent), followed by 90-99 (1.1 per cent) and 10-19 (5.1 per cent).

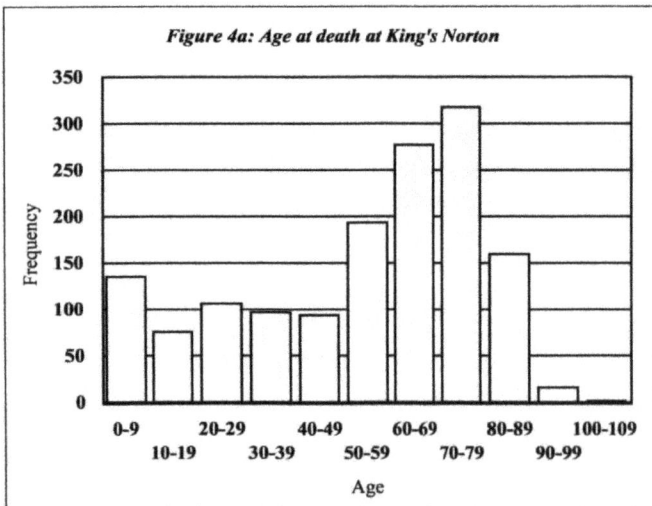

Figure 4a: Age at death at King's Norton

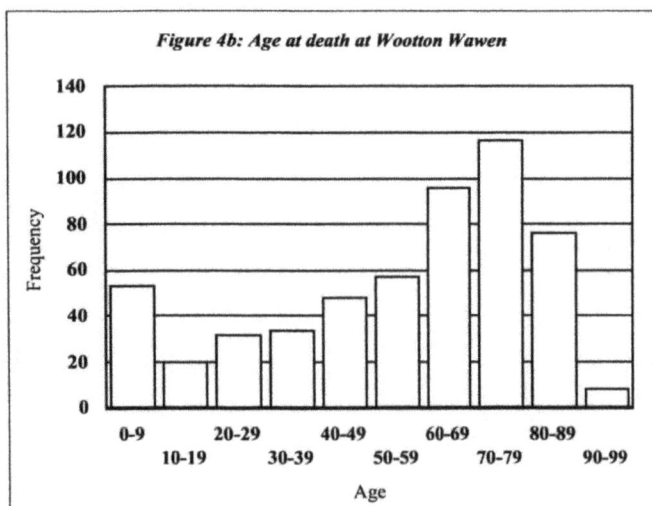

Figure 4b: Age at death at Wootton Wawen

The same analysis was done at Wootton Wawen and the results were strikingly similar. Figure 4b shows that the most frequently recorded age at death is 70-79 (21.6 per cent of the total), followed by 60-69 (17.7 per cent) and 80-89 (14 per cent). The least frequently recorded age at death is 90-99 (1.5 per cent) followed by 10-19 (3.7 per cent).

The results from the churchyard were compared with the burial registers to see how representative they are of the sorts of people living in the area at the time and whether they are historically reliable as a sample. The comparison of age at death figures could only be made between the years 1813 and 1940 because before this date age was not recorded in the burial registers. Over this period 1346 people from King's Norton could be used in the investigation of age at death, which was 14.5 per cent of the 9304 people recorded in the burial records[1] who could be used to investigate age at death. At Wootton Wawen the result was slightly higher with the results indicating that 430 people were still commemorated in the churchyard, which was 16.3 per cent of the 2637 people recorded in the burial registers[2] who could be used in this investigation. These are good sample sizes but were slightly disappointing because similar work at Baswich[3] found that 25 per cent of the people in the parish registers during the nineteenth century were still commemorated in the churchyard. It will be interesting to see how reliable these samples are.

The results for King's Norton are indicated in Figures 5a and 5b, which show that the results from the churchyard are fairly reliable and representative. The most frequently recorded ages at death in the registers are 0-9, 70-79, 60-69 and 50-59. This agrees with the results found from the memorials with the exception of the age group 0-9. The least frequently recorded ages at death in the registers are 90-99 and 10-19, which again mirrors the results from the yard. Surprisingly, the only person over the age of 100 still commemorated in the churchyard is one of only two people in the burial registers over the age of 100. More detailed comparison shows that in the burial registers 16.1 per cent of people died between the age of 70 and 79 compared with 22.2 per cent of the people in the churchyard, and 13 per cent of people died between the age of 60 and 69 compared with 19.3 per cent in the churchyard. When looking at the least frequently recorded age at death, 1 per cent of people died between the age of 90 and 109 in the registers compared with 1.26 per cent in the churchyard, and 5.04 per cent of people died aged 10-19 compared with 5.1 per cent in the churchyard. The biggest discrepancy is between the age 0 and 9. In the registers, 26.2 per cent of people died aged 0-9 compared with only 7.3 per cent in the churchyard.

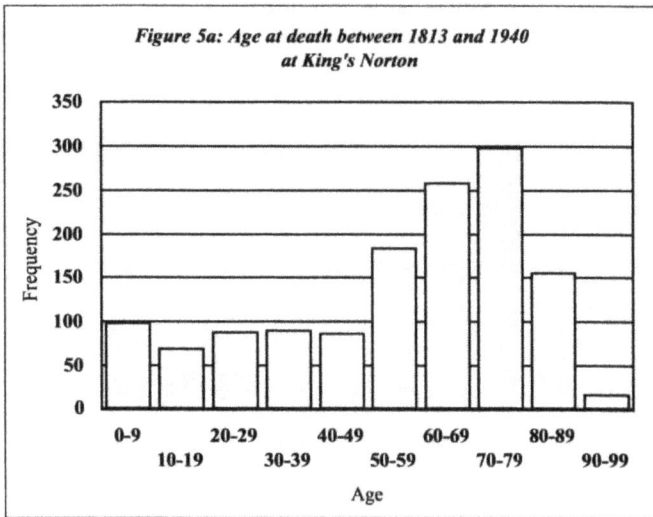

Figure 5a: Age at death between 1813 and 1940 at King's Norton

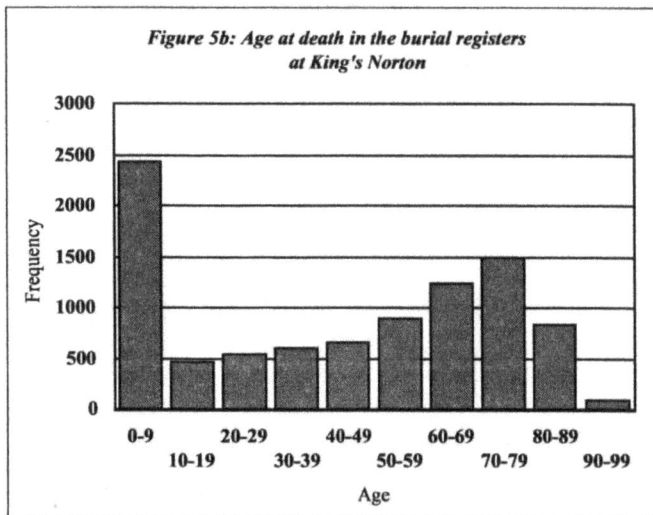

Figure 5b: Age at death in the burial registers at King's Norton

The results for Wootton Wawen are shown in Figures 6a and 6b. As at King's Norton, they appear to be fairly reliable and representative. In the registers the most frequently recorded ages at death are 0-9, 70-79, 60-69 and 80-89. These concur with the results from the churchyard with the exception of 0-9. The least frequently recorded ages at death in the registers are 90-109 and 10-19. It is the same in the churchyard except there is no one there aged between 100-109. More detailed comparison showed that in the burial registers 17 per cent of people died aged 70-79, compared with 23.7 per cent in the churchyard, and 13.2 per cent of the people died aged 60-69 compared with 19.3 per cent in the churchyard. When comparing the lowest figures recorded, 1.7 per cent of people died aged 90-109 compared to 1.9 per cent in the churchyard, and 4.7 per cent of people died aged 10-19 compared with 3.95 per cent in the churchyard. The biggest difference is between the ages 0-9. In the registers 25.2 per cent of people died aged 0-9, compared with only 4.7 per cent in the churchyard.

Analysis was done of the age at death of males compared to females. At King's Norton (Figures 7a) the male and female results are mostly the same. The main exception is in the age group 70-79 where more men died than women, and in the age group 80-99 where the number of women is slightly higher than that of men. The data from

the yard was compared with the burial registers (Figure 7b) and the results are similar. In the parish registers male and female results are mostly the same. More men are recorded than women in several of the age groups but more women are found than men in the highest age categories. The main discrepancy between the memorials and the burial registers is again in the age group 0-9, with this being the most frequently recorded age at death for both sexes in the registers but one of the least frequently recorded ages at death in the churchyard. There is also a small discrepancy in the age group 70-79 as in the churchyard more men are recorded than women, but in the registers the results for both sexes are similar.

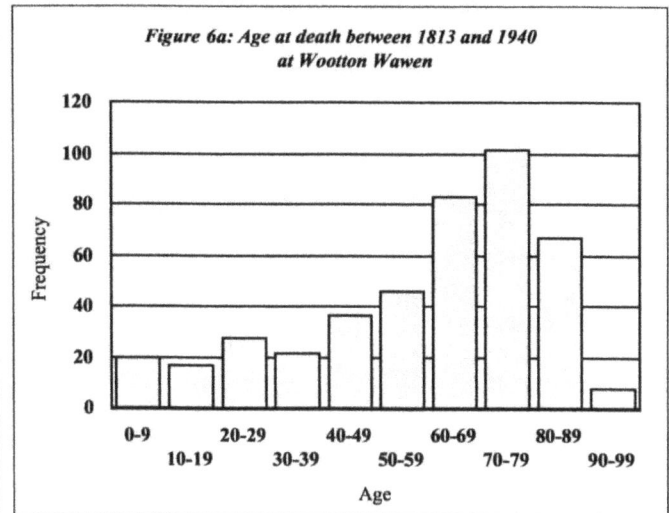

Figure 6a: Age at death between 1813 and 1940 at Wootton Wawen

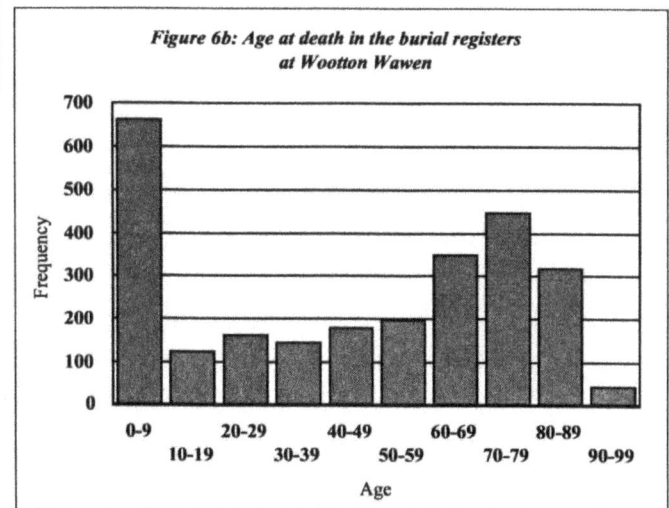

Figure 6b: Age at death in the burial registers at Wootton Wawen

At Wootton Wawen (Figure 8a), the male and female results are similar to those at King's Norton. There are slightly more men than women recorded in each age group except for small differences in the age groups 10-29 and 80-89 when the number of women is higher than that of men. These differences are mirrored in the burial registers (Figure 8b) and the results from the memorials appear to be fairly reliable. As found at King's Norton, the main discrepancy between the results from the memorials and the data from the parish registers is in the age group 0-9. At both churchyards there are more women recorded than men in the eldest age groups. This is also shown in the parish registers and may be because women generally lived to a greater age.

9

Figure 7a: Age at death of males compared to females at King's Norton

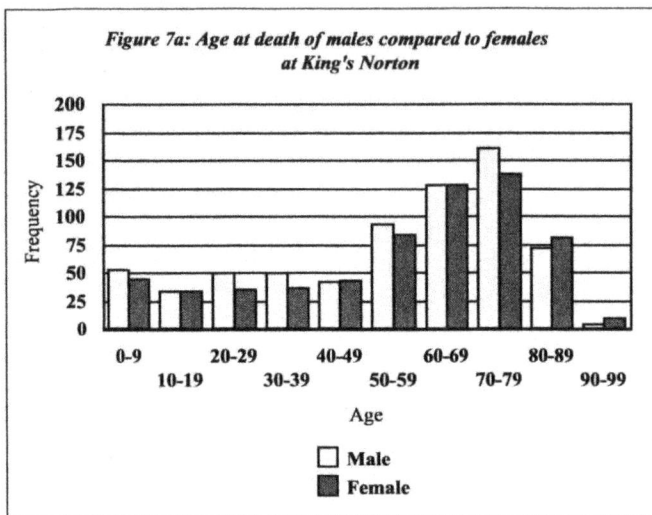

Figure 7b: Age at death of males compared to females in the burial registers at King's Norton

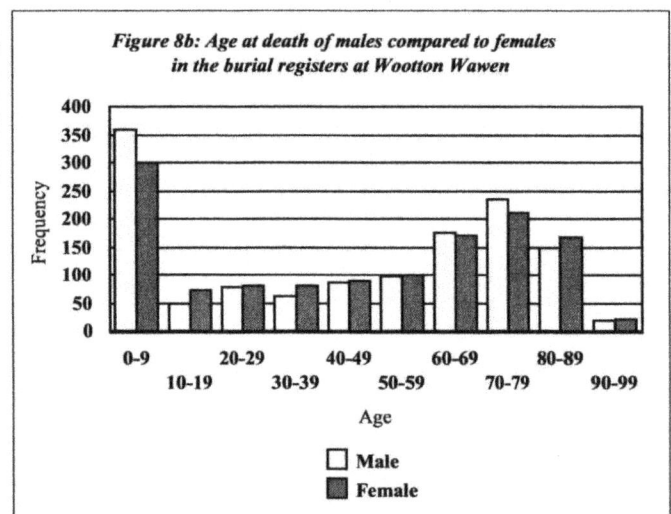

cent) followed by 60-69 (14.9 per cent), and the least frequently occurring was 90-99 (2 per cent) followed by 0-9 (6.4 per cent). In contrast, however, work by Rahtz[10] on church memorials at Wharram Percy found that although ten people lived to be over 70, the average age at death was 46. It is important to remember, however, that as only 31 stones were recorded in this study the sample is relatively very small. Rahtz himself argues that the sample of population in this study is demographically unrepresentative.[11]

Figure 8a: Age at death of males compared to females at Wootton Wawen

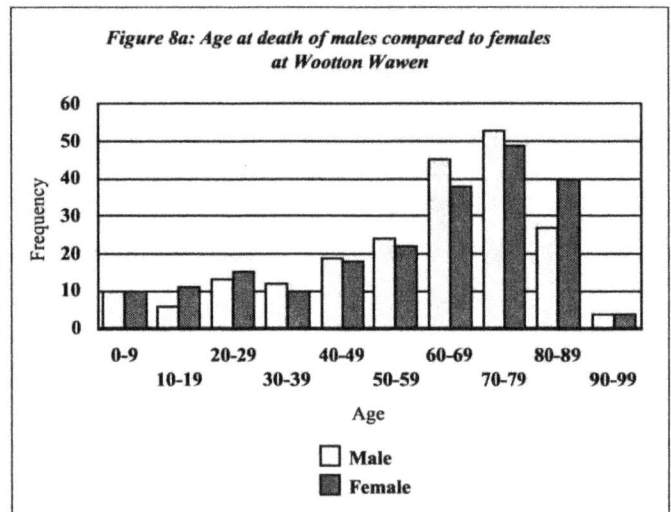

Figure 8b: Age at death of males compared to females in the burial registers at Wootton Wawen

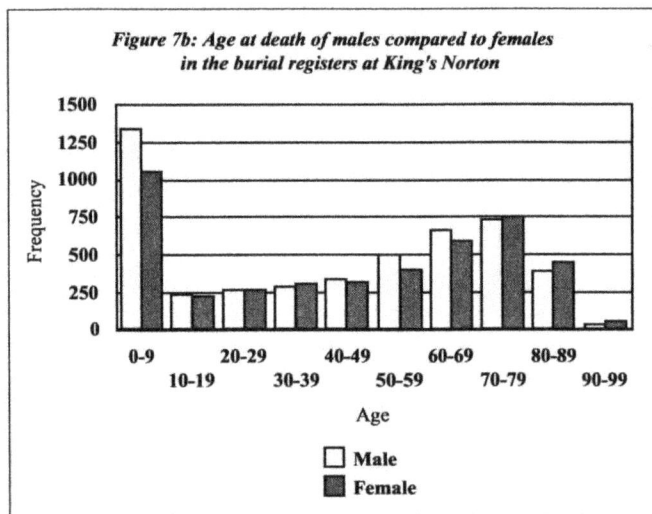

The results from both areas are quite surprising with age at death much higher than expected. François Bēdarida[4] puts average life expectancy in 1841 at between the age of 40 and 42. He argues that this remains fairly constant during the nineteenth century, rising to between 52 and 54 in 1910 and between 68 to 74 in 1960. The work of Porter[5] agrees with this, putting average life expectancy at 40 in 1850 and 44 in 1890. Similar results are also found in the work of Anderson,[6] who puts average age at death at 52 for males and 55 for females in 1911-1912 and at 66 and 72 respectively for 1950 to 1952. Trying to compare the results with national statistics is, however, difficult. In demography obtaining general figures can be hard because there are many regional differences. Local realities are more important, because for an individual the factors determining life and death are found only in the immediate environment.[7]

Comparing my results with regional studies is interesting. Wrigley and Schofield[8] place their life expectancy higher than the national averages suggested above, at between 55 and 60 between Elizabethan and Victorian times. The results from King's Norton and Wootton Wawen therefore show that the people were extremely healthy, with most people dying between the age of 60 and 79. Similar results were found during work in a rural area at Baswich churchyard, Staffordshire[9] where the most frequently occurring age at death was 70-79 (18.7 per

More detailed analysis was done comparing the age of death figures for the periods 1700-1799, 1800-1899 and 1900-1940. The number of people recorded between 1700 and 1799 is too small to be of statistical value, and so analysis has been concentrated on the period 1800 to 1940. Although the results are again extremely similar for King's Norton and Wootton Wawen, there are some small differences. Figure 9a shows the results from King's Norton. Between 1800 and 1899, the most frequently recorded age at death is 70-79 (18.9 per cent), followed by 60-69 (17.3 per cent) and 50-59 (12.4 per cent), and the least frequently recorded age at death, apart from five people over the age of 90, is 40-49 (5.5 per cent). Between 1900 and 1940 the most frequently recorded age at death is 70-79 (24.7 per cent) followed by 60-69 (21.2 per cent) and 50-59 (14.3 per cent). The least frequently recorded age at death, apart from 13 people aged over 90, is 10-19 (3.6 per cent) and 0-9 (5 per cent). These results indicate that life expectancy increased in King's Norton between 1800 and 1940 as a much higher number of people are recorded as dying between the age of 40 and 89, whereas there has been a reduction in the number of people dying between the age of 0 and 39, particularly in the age group 0-19.

1813 and 1899 the most frequently recorded age in the registers is 0-9 (32 per cent), followed by 70-79 (13.2 per cent) and 60-69 (11.2 per cent). The least frequently recorded ages at death are 90-109 (0.91 per cent) and 10-19 (5.9 per cent). Between 1900 and 1940 the most frequently recorded age at death is 70-79 (20 per cent), followed by 0-9 (18.4 per cent) and 60-69 (16.5 per cent). The least frequently recorded ages at death are 90-99 (1.2 per cent) and 10-19 (3.8 per cent). The results from the burial registers mirror the results from the yard and indicate that life expectancy increased in King's Norton between 1813 and 1940.

Detailed analysis was also done at Wootton Wawen and the results are shown in Figure 10a. As found at King's Norton, the results between 1700 and 1799 are too small to be of statistical value, and so analysis has been concentrated on the period 1800 to 1940. Between 1800 and 1899 the most frequently recorded age at death is 70-79 (22.3 per cent), followed by 60-69 (17.1 per cent) and 80-89 (12.9 per cent). The least frequently recorded age at death apart from three people aged between 90-99 is 10-19 (4.8 per cent). Between 1900 and 1940 the most frequently recorded age at death is 70-79 (28.3 per cent), followed by 60-69 (22.5 per cent) and 80-89 (21.7 per cent). The least frequently recorded are 0-9, 10-19 and 30-39 which each account for 1.4 per cent of the total. The only difference between the two areas therefore is that a slightly higher percentage of people lived longer in Wootton Wawen, particularly until their 80s. In King's Norton, the largest

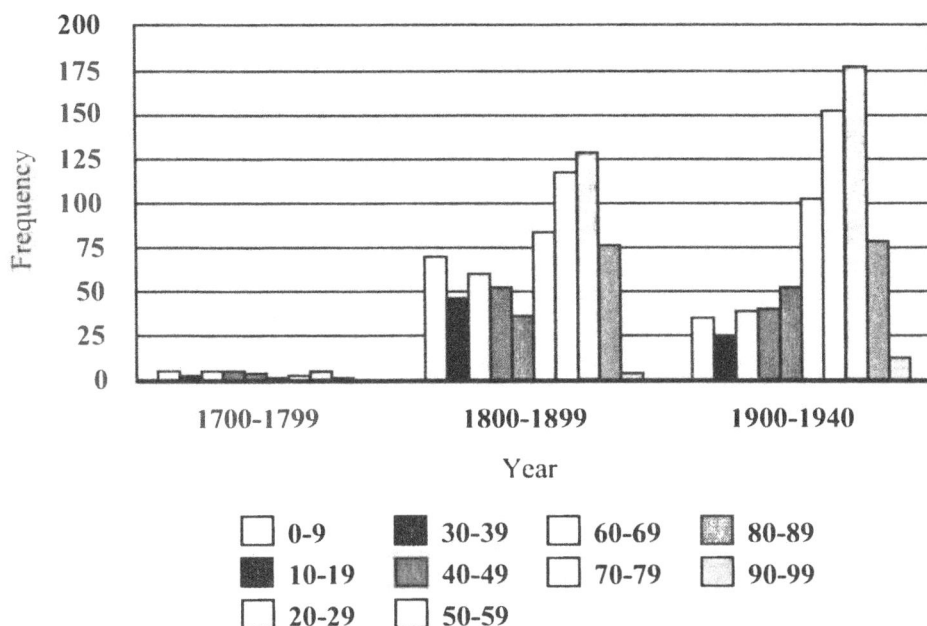

Figure 9a: Age at death 1700 to 1940 at King's Norton

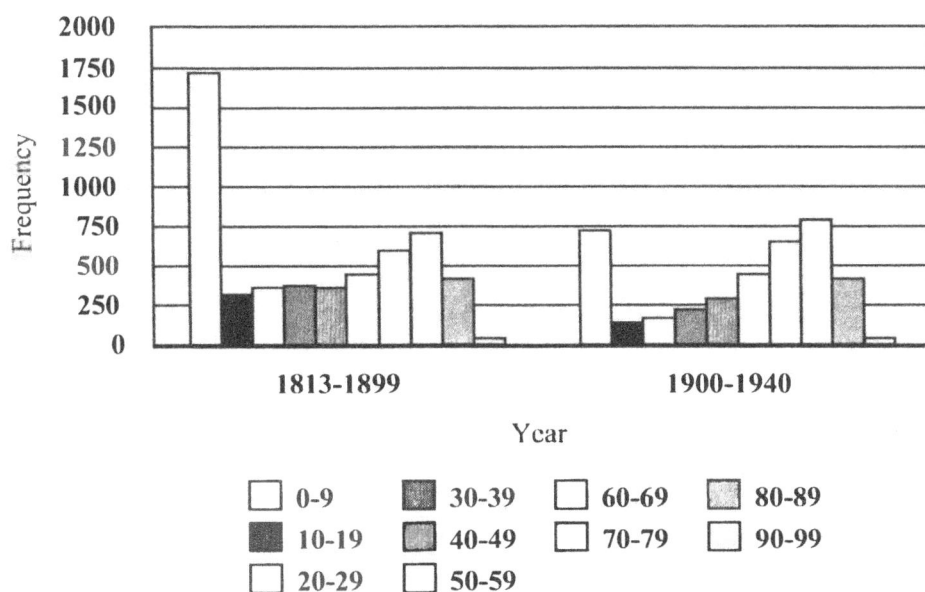

Figure 9b: Age at death 1813 to 1940 in the burial registers at King's Norton

Analysis of the burial registers between 1813 and 1940 shows that the data from the memorials is extremely accurate and representative (Figure 9b), with the main discrepancy again being in the age group 0-9. Between

number of people died aged between 60 and 79 but a lot also died in their 50s.

Figure 10a: Age at death 1700 to 1940 at Wootton Wawen

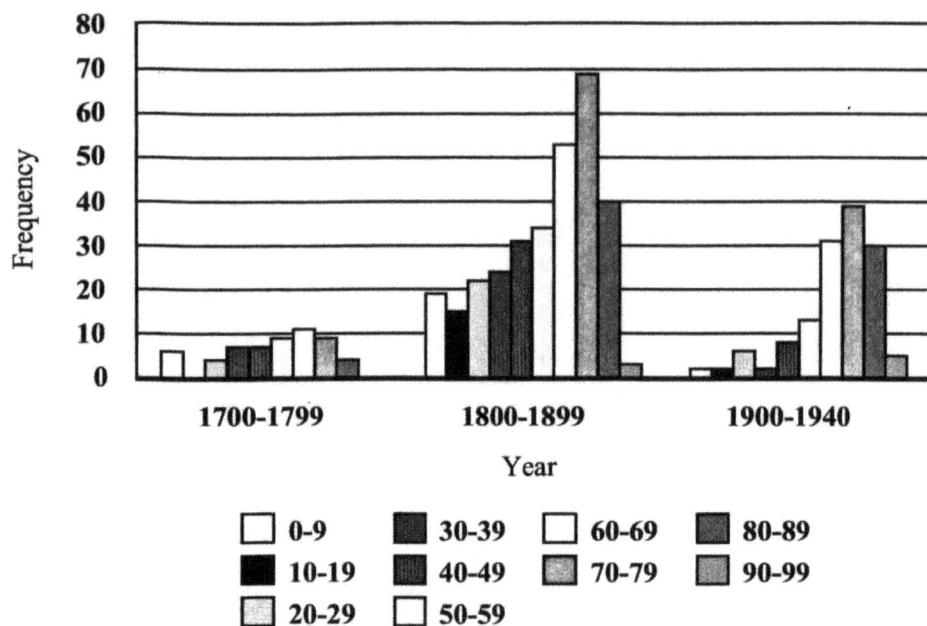

Figure 10a: Age at death 1700 to 1940 at Wootton Wawen

Figure 10b: Age at death 1813 to 1940 in the burial registers at Wootton Wawen

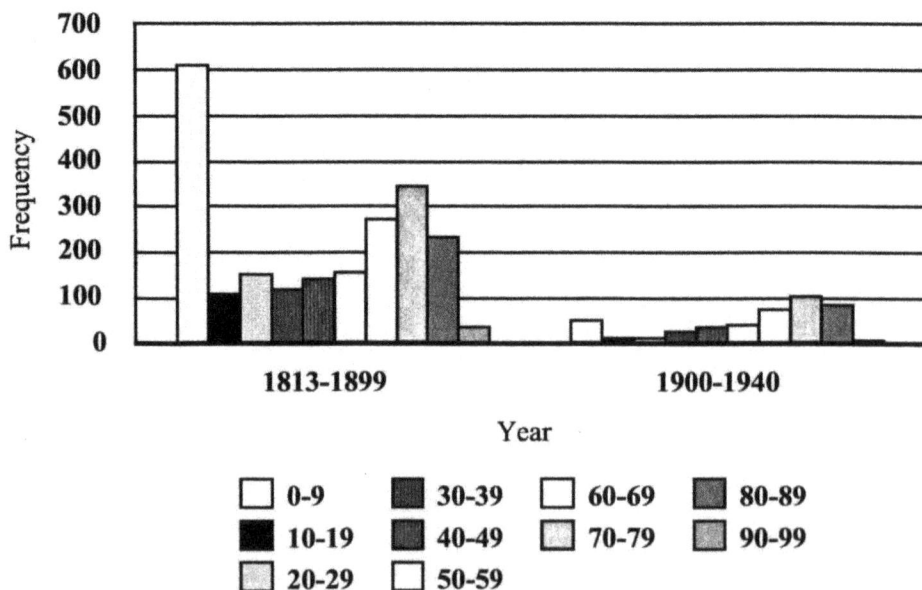

Figure 10b: Age at death 1813 to 1940 in the burial registers at Wootton Wawen

frequently recorded age at death is 70-79 (23.2 per cent), followed by 80-89 (18.8 per cent) and 60-69 (16.8 per cent). The least frequently recorded age at death is 90-99 (1.5 per cent), followed by 20-29 (2.7 per cent) and 10-19 (2.9 per cent). The data from the burial registers agrees with the results from the churchyard which indicate that life expectancy increased in Wootton Wawen. Age at death is similar at both King's Norton and Wootton Wawen with the only difference being that a slightly higher percentage of people lived longer in Wootton Wawen, into their 80s, whereas at King's Norton more people died in their 50s.

Changes in life expectancy over the period studied are analysed in more detail in Figures 11a and 12a, where people's ages at death are shown over time from 1800 to 1940. At King's Norton (Figure 11a) the data shows that as the decades pass, increasing percentages of people were dying between the age of 60 and 89. The number of people recorded between the age of 0 and 9 fluctuates widely during the nineteenth century and is still fluctuating slightly between 1900 and 1940, but there has been a clear fall in the number of deaths in this age range. In the age group 10-19, there have been fluctuating results throughout the period studied, but there is a definite fall in the number of deaths in this category from about 1880 onwards. The number of people dying in middle age also falls from the late nineteenth century.

Analysis of the burial registers at Wootton Wawen between 1813 and 1940 shows that the data from the memorials is fairly reliable with the main discrepancy again being found in the age group 0-9 (Figure 10b). Between 1813 and 1899 the most frequently recorded age at death is 0-9 (28 per cent), followed by 70-79 (15.7 per cent) and 60-69 (12.5 per cent). The least frequently recorded age at death is 90-109 (1.7 per cent) followed by 10-19 (5 per cent). Between 1900 and 1940 the most

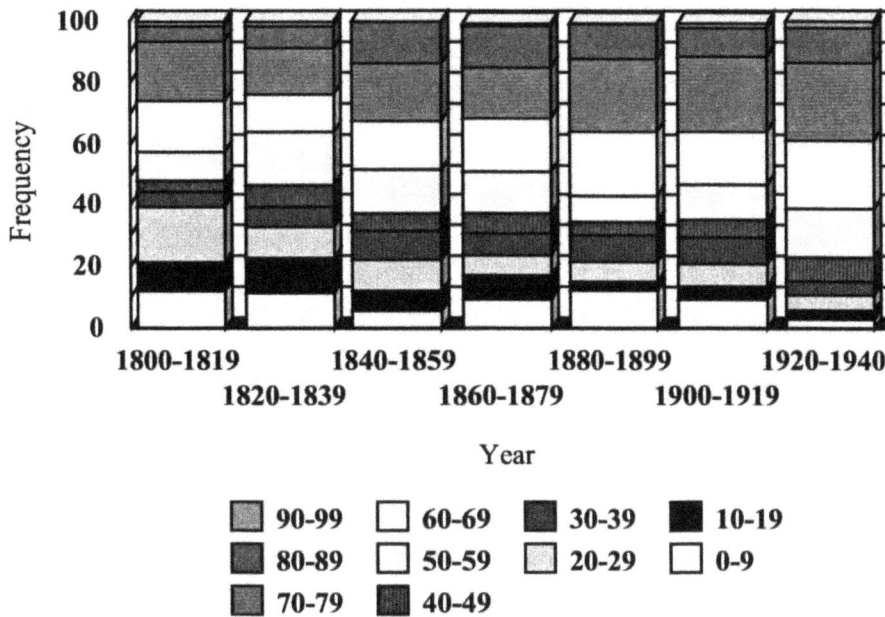

Figure 11a: Age at death over time at King's Norton

Frequency

90-99	60-69	30-39	10-19
80-89	50-59	20-29	0-9
70-79	40-49		

Age at death was also analysed over time at Wootton Wawen. The results from the churchyard show that over the years, ever fewer people were dying between the age of 0 and 59 (Figure 12a). The number of people dying between the age of 0 and 19 fell from about 1889 and the infant mortality rate dropped sharply after 1899. The number of people dying in middle age started to fall in the late nineteenth century and fell sharply after 1900. At Wootton Wawen ever more people were dying in the higher age categories, particularly 70-79 and increasingly 80-89.

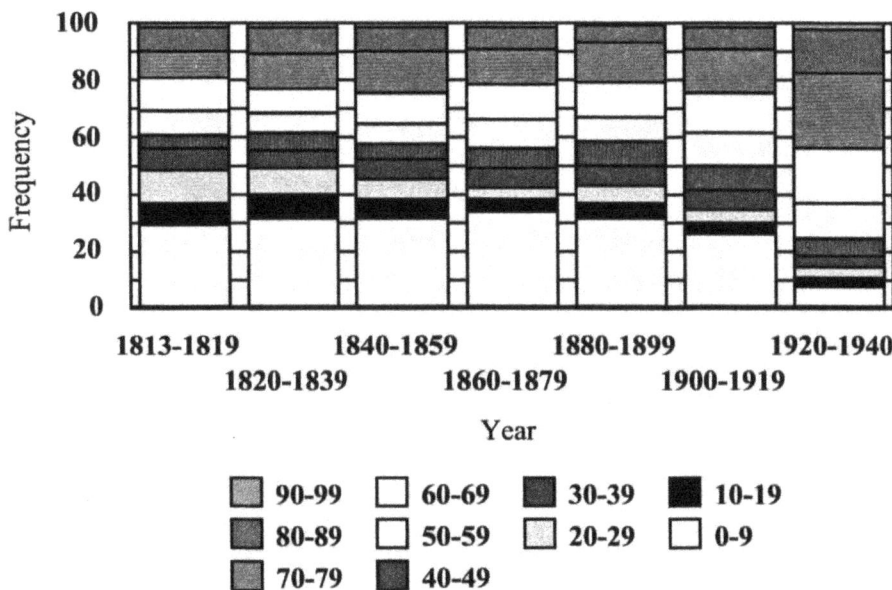

Figure 11b: Age at death over time in the burial registers at King's Norton

Frequency

90-99	60-69	30-39	10-19
80-89	50-59	20-29	0-9
70-79	40-49		

Analysis of the burial registers over time (Figure 12b) shows that the data from the grave memorials is extremely reliable and representative of the people living in the community during this period. The results mirror those from the churchyard, with ever more people dying aged 60 to 89, particularly in the higher age categories. The number of people dying between the ages of 10 and 59 fell during the nineteenth century and infant mortality remained high until the late nineteenth century and then dropped sharply.

Analysis of the burial registers over time at King's Norton (Figure 11b) shows that the results from the memorials are extremely accurate and representative. Over the period 1813 to 1940 the results from the parish registers concur with those from the churchyard showing that ever more people were dying between the age 50 and 89. Infant mortality remained high throughout the nineteenth century and there was only a sharp fall in this category in the period 1920 to 1940. Towards the end of the nineteenth century fewer people were dying aged 10-19 and less people were dying in middle age.

The results from King's Norton and Wootton Wawen agree with the results found in national figures on life expectancy. Harris[12] argues that there is a fall in the death rate of children and young women from the 1870s and of middle-aged people in the 1880s and 1890s. Infant mortality however remained high. Royle argues that infant mortality only fell from the start of the twentieth century when there is a downturn in infectious epidemic disease, which is coupled with an improvement in environment, care and nutrition.[13] The fall in infant mortality shown in the results at King's Norton and

Wootton Wawen may possibly be a result of these factors.

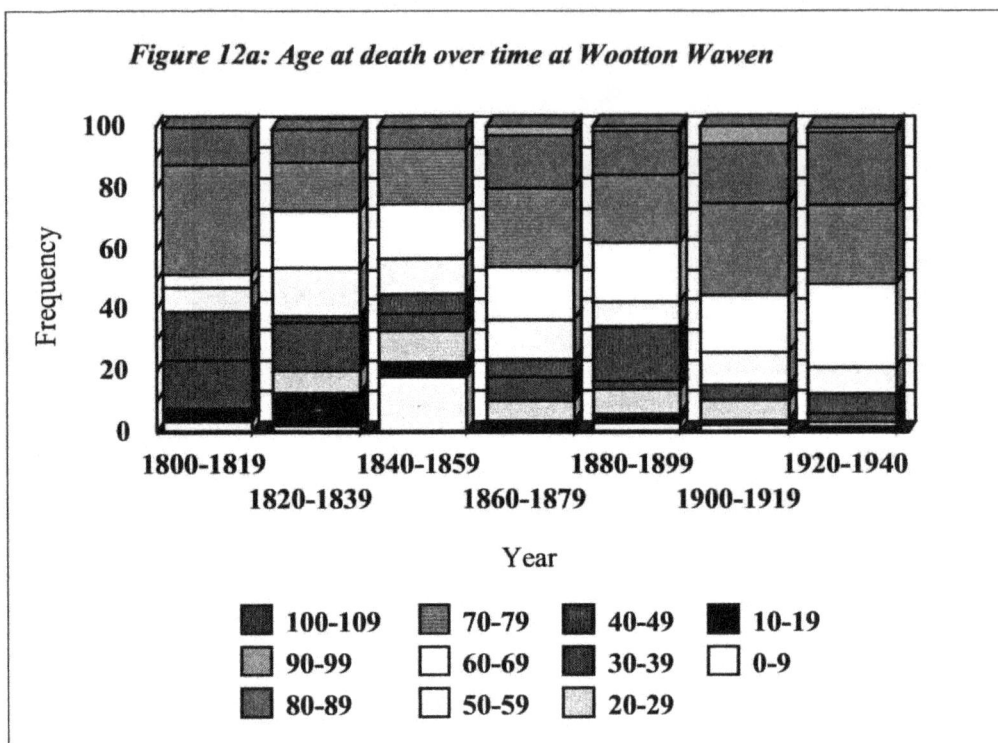

Figure 12a: Age at death over time at Wootton Wawen

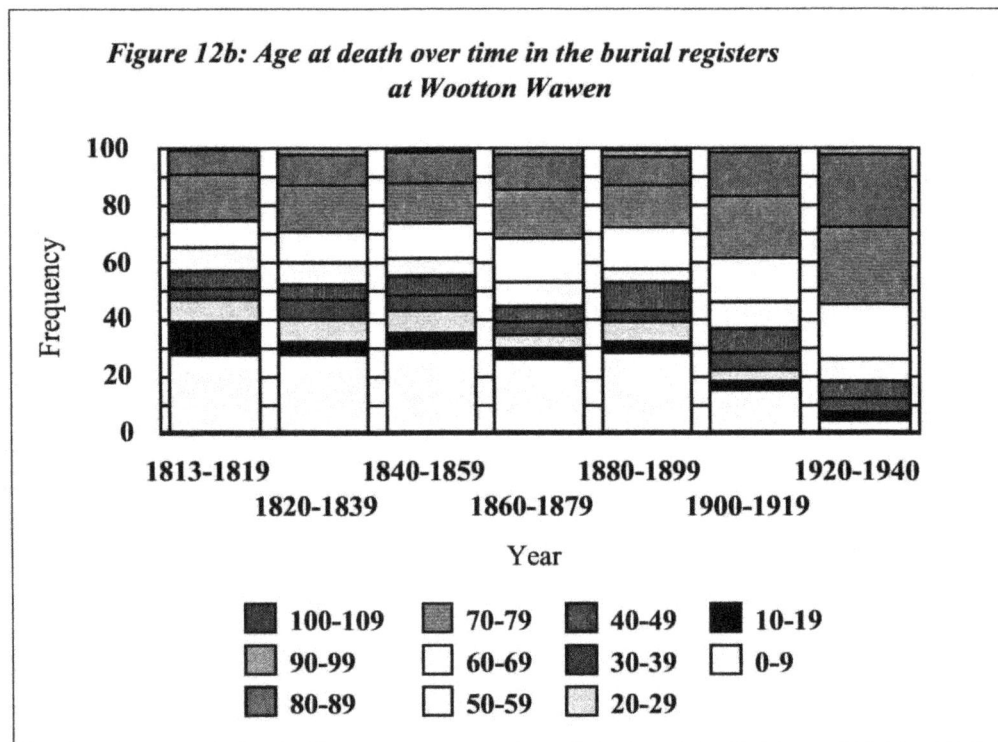

Figure 12b: Age at death over time in the burial registers at Wootton Wawen

and poor sanitation and housing which can lead to water-borne diseases such as Cholera, typhus and typhoid. For the majority of the period, the parish of King's Norton was still predominantly rural, which is likely to be the best explanation of the similarities between the ages at death when compared with Wootton Wawen. During the period 1800-1940, the only significant difference between the two areas is that a higher percentage of people live longer in Wootton Wawen, whereas in King's Norton, more people die between the age of 50 and 59. Even these differences are small, but can possibly be explained by the closeness of King's Norton to Birmingham. The death rate in Birmingham was extremely high, for example, between 1851 and 1860 it was at 26.3 per 1,000. This was significantly higher than the national average of 21.6 per 1,000, and infant mortality here was 40% higher than in most of the rest of the country.[15] There is no improvement in the death rate in this area till about 1870 when there starts to be an improvement in housing and sanitation and a reduction in infectious diseases. Over the period studied parts of King's Norton parish became ever more significantly affected by the urban growth of Birmingham. King's Norton itself was still very much a village and much of the parish was still under pasture and meadow but changes in transport in the nineteenth century[16] led to increasing contact with Birmingham. Consequently the trade and population of the parish increased enormously during the nineteenth century, and parts of the parish became residential suburbs. The most populous areas were those closest to Birmingham. This meant that more and more people who were buried in the yard were townspeople. From 1850 onwards there is also some

The analysis of the data over time has shown that throughout the entire period studied the results of age at death from King's Norton and Wootton Wawen are extremely similar. Rising life expectancy in both areas can best be explained by a reduction in deaths from infectious diseases, improving living standards and improvements in nutrition.[14] The death rate is usually found to be higher in urban areas particularly in cities and manufacturing areas because of environmental factors industry in the area with, for example, a metal company at Selly Oak, India rubber works at Lifford Mills and a screw works at Stirchley.[17] Even as the area becomes increasingly in touch with Birmingham and the population grew in the parish, this does not necessarily mean that there will be a worsening death rate as population growth can be due to natural increase, young immigrants and migration of people out of the city into the suburbs, which does not worsen the death rate.

The death rate in King's Norton is extremely low. Between 1851 and 1860 the death rate was only 17 per 1,000.[18] This shows why age at death is so similar between King's Norton and the deeply rural Wootton Wawen. Even by the time King's Norton enters the boundaries of the city of Birmingham in 1911, there is no major difference between the ages at death of the two increasingly different socio-economic environments. This is because as parts of the parish of King's Norton became increasingly more urban, the gap between urban and rural death rates was closing until in the twentieth century it disappeared completely.[19]

The comparison of the data from the memorial stones with the parish registers has shown the grave memorials to be fairly reliable and representative of the communities of King's Norton and Wootton Wawen during the nineteenth and early twentieth centuries. The main inconsistency, between the churchyards and the parish registers is between the age of 0 and 9. Even the high results in the registers may not be a valid representation of infant mortality, however, because many children died before baptism and it is not clear how many of these are recorded in the parish registers.[20] In the churchyards 0-9 was one of the lowest recorded ages at death found but during the nineteenth century approximately one quarter of children died before the age of ten and in their first year 150 per 1000 infants died.[21] The high incidence of infant mortality is not represented in surviving infant commemoration and there is a poor showing of the youngest age group in grave memorials. At a similar study in Spitalfields during an excavation of a burial crypt, children were found to be under-represented for the entire period of crypt use.[22] The same problem was found in similar studies elsewhere such as at St Bride's Church, Fleet Street, London.[23] Here, it was found that children represented 6.6 per cent of the total, which was not consistent with expected mortality rates of the time. At Baswich, the results were slightly lower with children representing 6.37 per cent of the total.[24] Compared to other areas, both King's Norton and Wootton Wawen churchyards have a large number of children recorded. At King's Norton the age group 0-9 represent 9.2 per cent of the total number of people recorded, and at Wootton Wawen it represents 9.8 per cent.

There are problems when trying to use memorial stones to look at life expectancy. The results may not show a true picture for several reasons: Firstly, the older, more respected, wealthy people may be the only ones to get memorial stones or they may have had stones of better quality which were perhaps more durable with a better chance of survival. Secondly, infants and children may

have had only a small memorial, a temporary one or none at all. The problem of the lack of commemoration of infants is seen quite clearly in King's Norton and Wootton Wawen churchyards. Even when the death of a child was commemorated on a stone many people simply recorded the death as a daughter or son who died in their infancy and the date of death and the age of the child were often not recorded Although it undoubtedly causes problems when trying to use memorial stones as evidence of demography, this lack of commemoration in the youngest age group provides valuable evidence of attitudes to children. It may seem heartless that there was often no permanent memorial for children, but in a period when infant mortality was so high the death of a child was almost expected. Grief at the loss of babies and children affected hundreds of thousands of people each year, but burial was an expensive business and it was probably only the very well off who could easily afford to put up lasting monuments to their children.

Month of death

The inscriptions were used to investigate time of year of death. The number of people recorded between 1700 and 1799 is too small to be of statistical value, and so analysis has been concentrated on the period 1800 to 1940. During this time at King's Norton, month of death was indicated for 1439 people, 95 per cent of the 1513 people recorded in the yard. At Wootton Wawen the result was even higher, with month of death indicated for 464 (99 per cent) people out of 467 recorded during this period. The results for King's Norton are shown in Figure 13a. From the line graph it appears that the highest number of deaths occurred in late winter[25] and early spring with most deaths (in decreasing order of magnitude, as always hereafter) in January and February and less prominent peaks in April and March. Fewest deaths occurred in summer months, particularly in July and August. The results for Wootton Wawen are shown in Figure 14a. From the line graph it appears that most people died in late winter and late autumn with high numbers of deaths occurring in February, January and November. Smaller peaks in April and August indicate that many people also died in spring and summer. Fewest deaths occurred in July, and September.

The results from the memorials were compared with the burial registers to see how reliable and representative of the people living in the community during this period the grave memorials are. In King's Norton churchyard the month of death of 1439 people could be analysed. This was 14.5 per cent of the 9921 from the parish registers who could be used to investigate month of death between 1800 and 1940. The results from Wootton Wawen were compared with the burial registers (Figure 14b) to see how reliable they are. In the churchyard, the month of death of 464 people could be analysed. This was 15 per cent of the 3045 people recorded in the burial registers who could be used to look at month of death.

Figure 13b shows the results from the parish registers at King's Norton. In the churchyard (Figure 13a) there were prominent peaks in January, February and April, and in the parish registers there were peaks in March, February and January. Fewest deaths occurred in (in increasing order of magnitude, as always hereafter) July, August, October and September in the churchyard compared with September, August and July in the burial registers. The sample from the yard was therefore fairly reliable in showing that most deaths occurred in late winter and early spring and the least in midsummer.

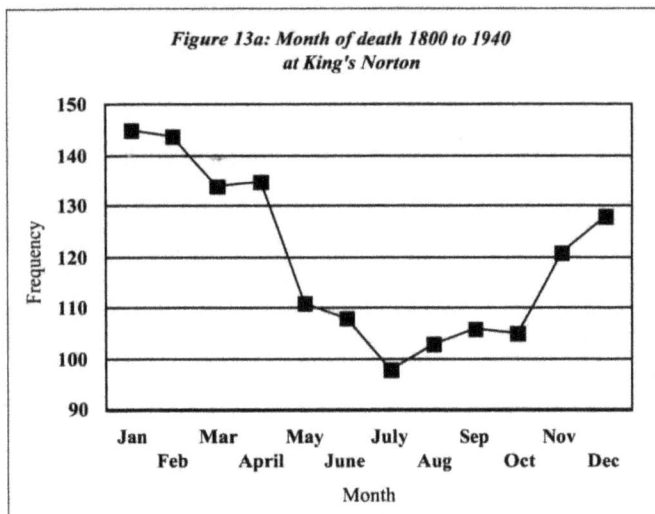

Figure 13a: Month of death 1800 to 1940 at King's Norton

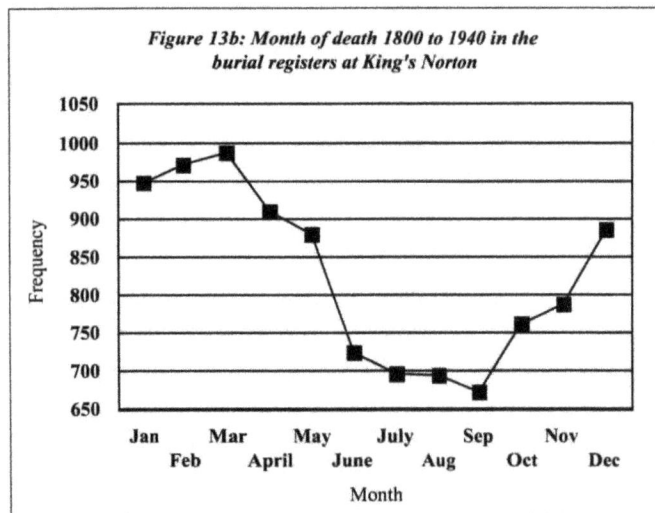

Figure 13b: Month of death 1800 to 1940 in the burial registers at King's Norton

Figure 14b shows the results from the parish registers at Wootton Wawen. In the churchyard (Figure 14a) the most prominent peaks were in February, January and November, with smaller peaks in April and August. In the parish registers the most prominent peaks were in January, April, February and March. In the churchyard the lowest number of deaths occurred in July and September and in the burial registers the lowest number of deaths occurred in July, September and August. The results from the churchyard are again fairly accurate in indicating that most deaths were in winter and early spring and the least in midsummer and autumn. The main discrepancies are in the months of August and November where the results from the churchyard show that they were two of the highest months of deaths recorded, however, in the burial registers they were two of the lowest months of deaths recorded.

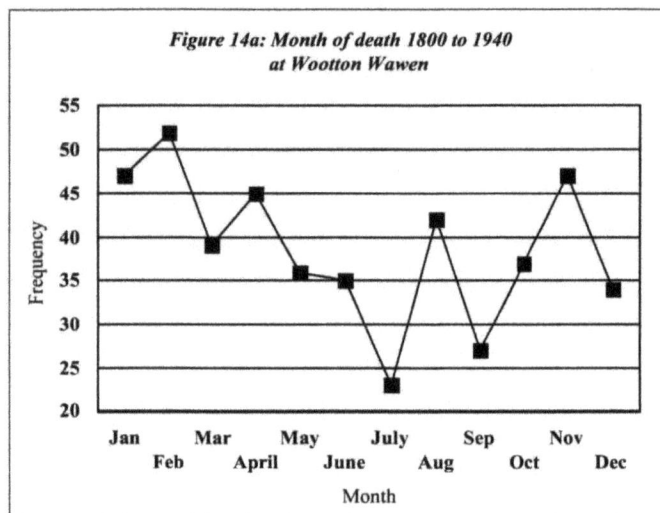

Figure 14a: Month of death 1800 to 1940 at Wootton Wawen

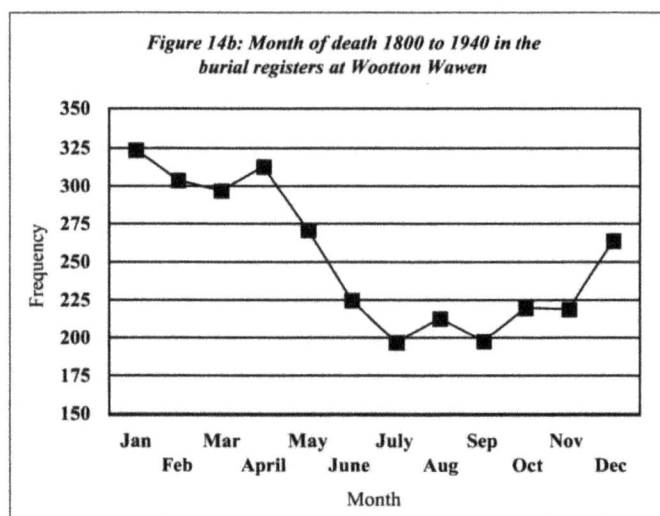

Figure 14b: Month of death 1800 to 1940 in the burial registers at Wootton Wawen

The results from King's Norton fit the Wrigley-Schofield model perfectly. They argue that most deaths occurred in late winter and early spring and the fewest in midsummer. More specifically their findings showed that the largest numbers of people died in March, April and January, fell from March to a minimum in the summer, with a trough in July, and rose again from July to January.[26] At King's Norton the number of deaths fell from April to a minimum in July and then rose again from July onwards except for a slight dip in October.

The results from King's Norton also match the results found during a similar investigation at Baswich, Staffordshire.[27] Here, the highest number of deaths occurred in early spring and winter with fewest deaths in summer. The number of deaths fell from a March peak to a trough in July, and then slowly rose again throughout the winter. Although the peaks are in different months at Wootton Wawen, the results are similar to King's Norton and Baswich as most deaths occurred in the very late winter and early spring. The main difference between the two areas appeared to be a peak of deaths in August at Wootton Wawen that was not found at King's Norton. The discrepancy between the memorials and the registers, however, shows that the month of death at King's Norton and Wootton Wawen is even more similar than the memorials indicated. This can be explained by both areas being predominantly rural for most of the period studied.

16

Apart from in cities with poor sanitation, which helped increase the death rate in the summer, Wrigley and Schofield[28] found that most areas in England and also in northern continental Europe, where the climate was similar, had most deaths occurring in spring and winter and the least in summer. The results from King's Norton and Wootton Wawen agree with these findings.

The month of death of males compared to females was analysed. At King's Norton (Figure 15a) more males died in winter than in any other season, with the highest number dying in February. There were also a large number of deaths in November and March. The lowest number of male deaths occurred midsummer, with the lowest point in August. More females died in winter than in any other season, with peaks in January and December. A peak in April indicates that there were also a large number of deaths in spring. The lowest number of deaths occurred in late spring, autumn and midsummer, with low points in May, November and July.

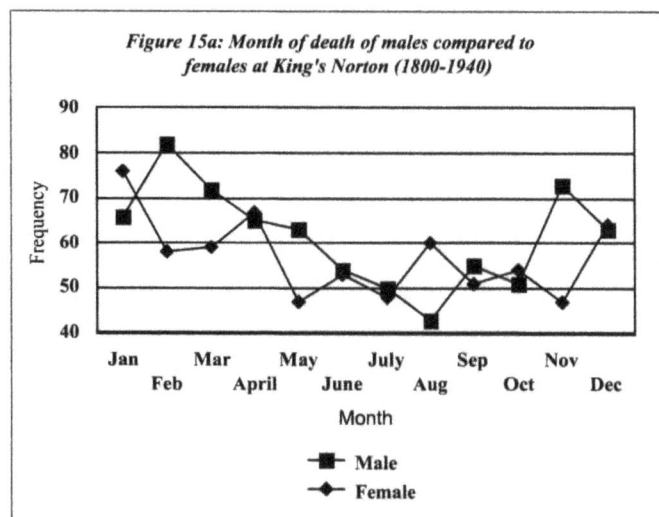

Figure 15a: Month of death of males compared to females at King's Norton (1800-1940)

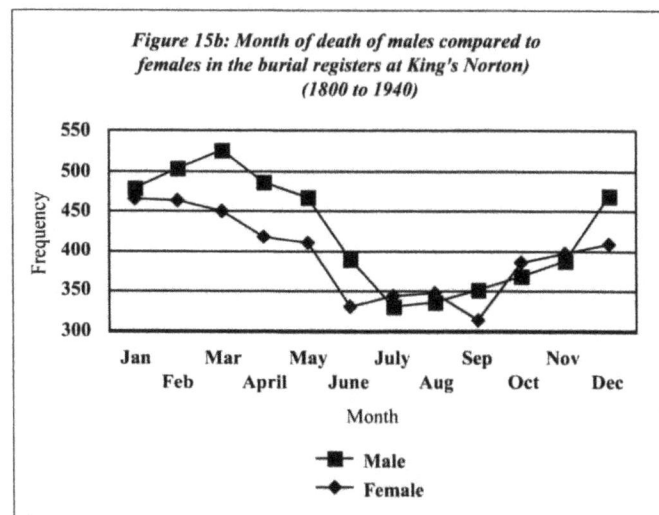

Figure 15b: Month of death of males compared to females in the burial registers at King's Norton) (1800 to 1940)

The results from the churchyard were compared with the parish registers to see how reliable they are (Figure 15b). The parish registers show that the results from the memorials are again fairly accurate, with most male deaths in spring and late winter in March, February and April, and fewest deaths in midsummer, in July and August. There were more female deaths in winter and late

spring than in any other season, with peaks in January, February and March. The lowest number of female deaths occurred in summer and autumn with fewest deaths in September, June and August. Comparing the month-of-death statistics for men and women shows that for both sexes most deaths occurred in winter and fewest in summer, although the months with the most male and female deaths were different from each other. Both sexes may have been hit by respiratory disease in the winter, but they may also have died in spring, possibly as a result of the diminishing food supply.

At Wootton Wawen (Figure 16a), more males died in winter than in any other season with a peak in January. There were also peaks in midsummer in August, and smaller peaks in February, April and October. Fewer males died in June than at any other time, with low numbers of deaths also occurring in September and July. More females died in winter and late autumn than at any other period, with the highest peaks in February and November. The lowest number of female deaths occurred in July, September and December.

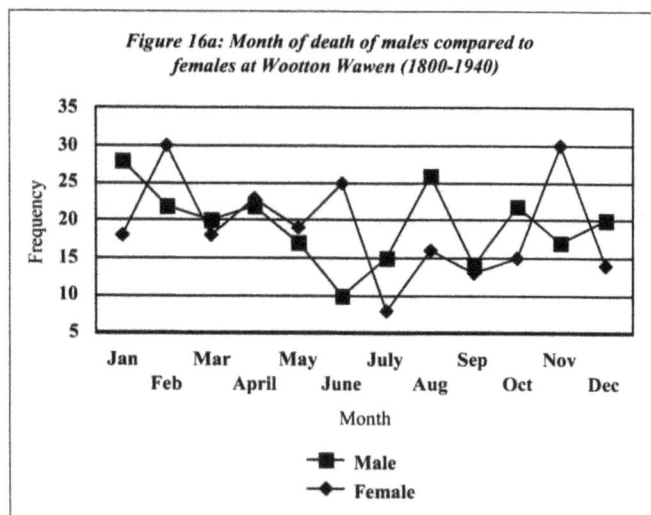

Figure 16a: Month of death of males compared to females at Wootton Wawen (1800-1940)

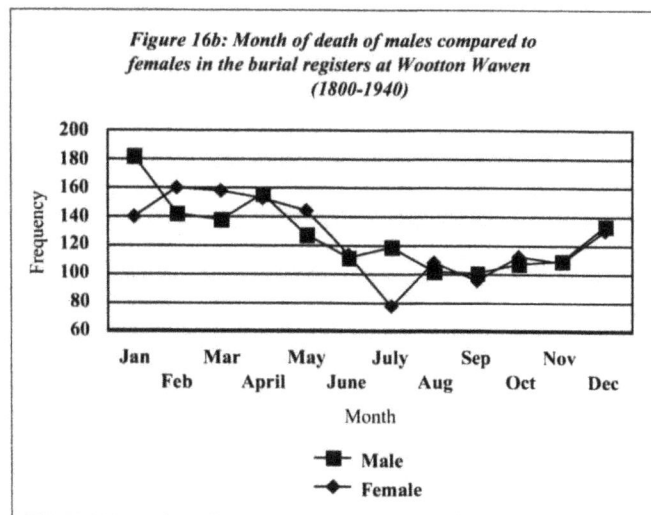

Figure 16b: Month of death of males compared to females in the burial registers at Wootton Wawen (1800-1940)

The results from Wootton Wawen were compared with the parish registers to see how reliable they are (Figure 16b). The highest number of male deaths occurred in winter and spring, with peaks in January, April, February and March. Fewest male deaths occurred in summer and autumn with low points in August and September. More females died in late winter and spring than in any other season, with most deaths occurring in February, March, April and May. Fewest female deaths occurred in summer and autumn in July and September. The results from Wootton Wawen show that the time of year of death of males and females is similar with most people dying in late winter and early spring and fewest people dying in summer and autumn. The results are similar to those from King's Norton and suggest that the people of Wootton Wawen were also affected by respiratory diseases and a diminishing food supply. The main discrepancy between the data from the churchyards and the parish registers is that the memorials indicate that a high number of males died in August and this is not shown in the parish registers.

The month of death in the churchyards was analysed according to age group. The results for King's Norton are shown in Figure 17a. The line graph shows that for the age group 0-19 there were peaks in March, February and August, with fewest deaths occurring in May, October and June. The data from the memorials suggests that people aged 0-19 were susceptible to respiratory diseases, but there was also a peak in August, which possibly shows that they were affected by gastric diseases. The results from the registers (Figure 17b) also indicate that people aged 0-19 were susceptible to respiratory disease in the winter with most deaths occurring in late winter and early spring with peaks in February and March. The main discrepancy between the results from the churchyard and the parish registers is that the memorials show a high number of deaths occurring in August but this is one of the lowest recorded months of death in the registers. This suggests that children aged between 0 and 9 at King's Norton were not as heavily affected by gastric diseases as the results from the churchyard first seemed to indicate. The results in this age group have possibly been distorted because of the lack of surviving infant commemoration in the churchyard.

These results were compared with the age group 20-59 where the highest number of deaths occurred in winter and spring in January and May and fewest deaths occurred in July, August and September. The comparison from the parish registers shows the results from the churchyard for this age group are fairly reliable, with most deaths occurring in winter with peaks in January and December and fewest deaths in early autumn and summer in September and August.

The month of death for the age group 60-99 was also analysed. The results for this age group are similar to those for people aged 20-59 with the highest number of deaths occurring in winter and spring in February, December and April, and the lowest in summer in July, June and August. The results from the parish registers mirror the results from the grave memorials. In the age group 60-99, most deaths occurred in winter and early spring in April, December, January and February and the lowest number of deaths occurred in the summer. There is a sharp fall in the number of deaths from March to the lowest point in midsummer and the number of deaths then rises toward the end of the year. In the churchyard

there is a fall in the number of deaths in the age group 60-99 from April to a trough in July and the number of deaths then slowly rises to a peak in December.

The results indicate that in King's Norton the age groups 20-59 and 60-99 predominantly die in late winter and early spring, which suggests that these people were susceptible to respiratory diseases, which mainly occurred in winter. The impact of these diseases could be exacerbated during this season by cold temperatures.[29] Deaths occurring in late winter could also be because of nutritional problems, as people could not fend off disease. The lowest number of deaths in the age group 20-99 occurred in mid-summer, which suggests that these people were less susceptible to water and food borne diseases which could be worsened by hot temperatures.[30]

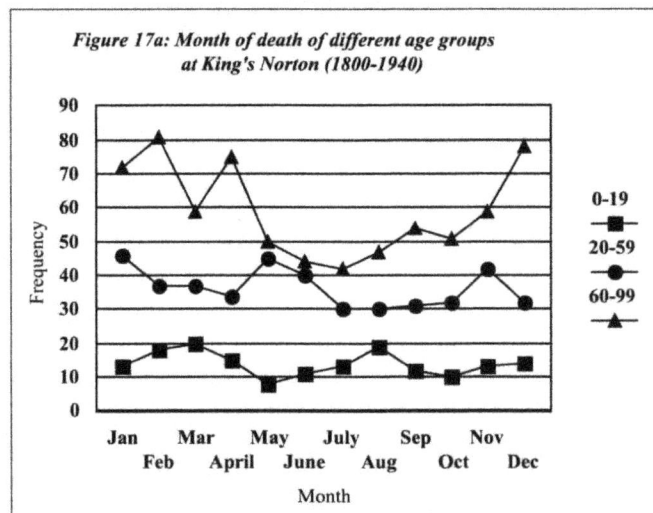

Figure 17a: Month of death of different age groups at King's Norton (1800-1940)

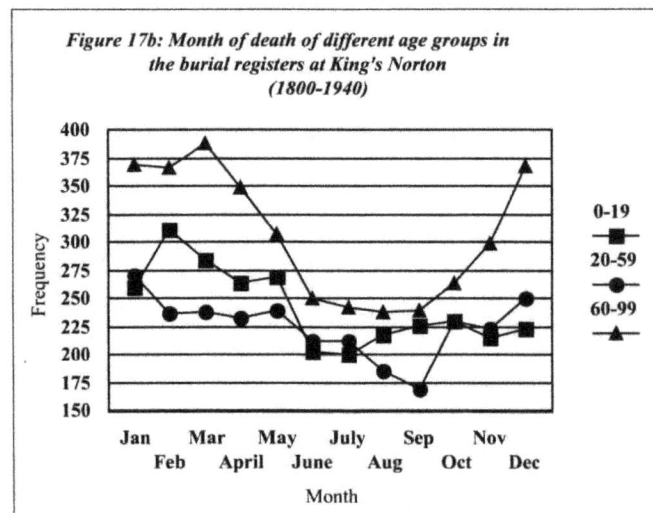

Figure 17b: Month of death of different age groups in the burial registers at King's Norton (1800-1940)

The month of death in Wootton Wawen churchyard was also analysed according to age group and the results are shown in Figure 18a. In the age group 0-19 the highest number of deaths occurred in August and May and the lowest number in July. The peaks at Wootton Wawen concur with results found at Spitalfields, where most children died in the months of August and November.[31] The results are also similar to those found at King's Norton for this age group, but it is important to remember that so few memorials survive for children that the results of those that have may be distorted. This is confirmed by a comparison with the parish registers (Figure 18b) which shows that the majority of children aged 0-9 actually died in winter and spring in April, March and February and fewest deaths occurred in July, September and November. This suggests that the children in Wootton Wawen were not as heavily affected by water and food borne diseases in the summer as the results in the churchyard first seemed to indicate. This also helps to explain why there was a discrepancy in the month of august between the memorials and parish registers in the analysis of total month of death and month of death of males and females.

The results for the age group 0-19 were compared with the age group 20-59, where the greatest number of deaths occurred in October, April, February and January. The lowest number of deaths occurred in September, June and July. These results are similar to those found at King's Norton for this age group, with the people arguably being affected by respiratory diseases and a diminishing food supply. Death as a result of malnutrition often occurred many months after the diminishing of the food supply.[32] The results from Wootton Wawen in this age group are slightly less reliable than at King's Norton as the memorials show a high number of deaths in October but in the parish registers October is one of the lowest recorded months of death. Apart from this discrepancy, however, the results from the parish registers agree with the data from the churchyard showing that most deaths in the age group 20-59 occurred in winter and spring and fewest deaths in summer.

The month of death was also analysed for the age group 60-99. The highest number of deaths occurred in late winter in February with smaller peaks in November and January, and the lowest number of deaths occurred in July, September and August. Again there is a slight discrepancy between the memorials and the parish registers with the results from the churchyard showing a peak in November but the parish registers only showing a slight rise in the number of deaths from September onwards. Overall, however, the data from the parish registers shows that the results from the grave memorials are fairly reliable with the highest number of deaths in late winter with a peak in January and fewest deaths in summer in September, July and August. The elderly population of Wootton Wawen were presumably affected by respiratory diseases in the cold winter months which could prove fatal to infants, the elderly and the weak.

When investigating age at death and month of death the comparison with the parish registers has shown that there are a couple of noticeable differences between the data from the memorials and the results from the burial registers. This is not surprising as even between 1900 and 1940 the memorials represent only a small percentage of the people buried in the churchyard during this period. A close match between the results from the churchyard and the parish registers was never expected and therefore the general tendency for the two to match indicates that the data is a more reliable and representative source of the sorts of people living in the community at the time than anticipated.

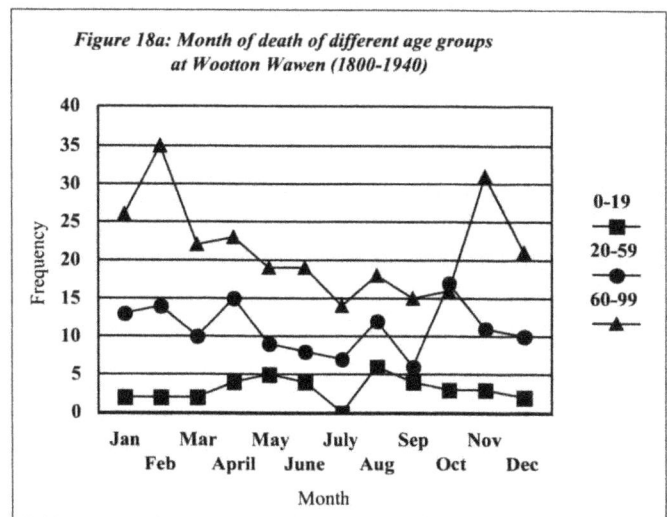

Figure 18a: Month of death of different age groups at Wootton Wawen (1800-1940)

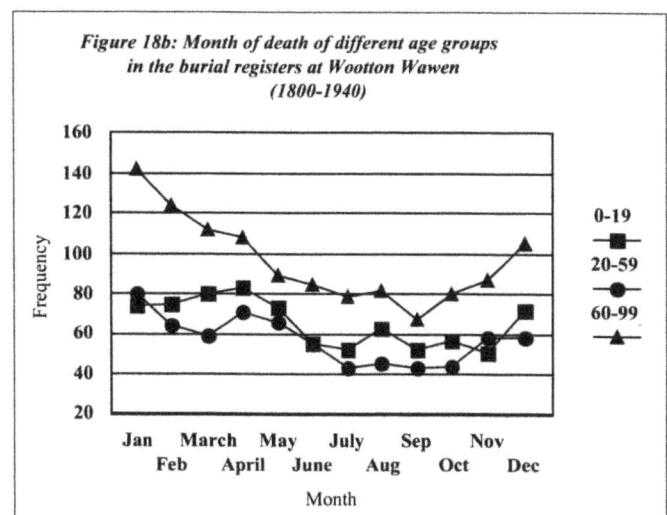

Figure 18b: Month of death of different age groups in the burial registers at Wootton Wawen (1800-1940)

Cause of death

Very few memorials indicate the cause of death. Throughout a survey of 389 memorials at Baswich there was not a single inscription recording the cause of death.[33] At King's Norton, only 11 of the memorials indicated the cause of death, with nine of them recording people who had died during war. The other two memorials indicated deaths due to illness and childbirth. At Wootton Wawen only 8 memorials record the cause of death of the deceased. Again war is found on three stones and illness on two. More unusual causes of death were found at Wootton Wawen with one man dying from shock and another dying from a fall from scaffolding. The final memorial indicates the cause of death of James Boeter (MA46) who was a steward and keeper of the hounds to William Somerville and died after being wounded internally when his horse fell in the hunt in 1719.

The memorial stones from King's Norton and Wootton Wawen have been useful for analysing age at death and season of death. Chapter 2 will look at a number of socio-economic and cultural aspects of the data which the memorials contain.

[1] Birmingham Reference Library. Registers for burials dating from 1546-1844 are transcribed in, *Registers of the Church of St. Nicholas, King's Norton, Worcestershire. Part three: marriages 1546-1754, burials 1546-1791* (1983) and *Registers of the Church of St. Nicholas, King's Norton, Worcestershire. Part two: baptisms and burial 1792-1844, marriages 1754-1837* (1981). Later registers are on microfilm in the Genealogy Department, EP4/2/4/2-EP4/2/4/6 for years 1844 to1944.

[2] These are held on microfilm at Warwickshire Record Office, DR195/2-DR195/4 for years 1700 to 1812, DR195/13 for 1813-1869, and DR740/3 for 1869-1979.

[3] I. Shorters, 'A study of the grave memorials of Holy Trinity Church, Baswich, Staffordshire' (University of Birmingham, unpublished BA dissertation, 2000), p. 12, cited hereafter as Shorters, 'Baswich'

[4] F. Bēdarida, *A Social History of England 1851-1990* (1991), p. 14

[5] R. Porter, ed., *Disease, Medicine and Society in England, 1550-1860* (1993), p. 61, cited hereafter as Porter, *Disease, Medicine and Society*

[6] M. Anderson, 'The social implications of demographic change', in ed. F. M. L. Thompson, *The Cambridge Social History of Britain 1750-1950. Volume 2: People and their Environment* (1990), pp. 1-71 (p. 16)

[7] P. Laslett, 'Introduction: The Numerical Study of English Society', in ed. E. A. Wrigley, *An Introduction to English Historical Demography: From the Sixteenth to the Nineteenth Century* (1966), pp. 18-19

[8] E. A. Wrigley and R. S. Schofield, *The Population History of England, 1541-1871. A Reconstruction* (1981), p. 453, cited hereafter as Wrigley and Schofield, *Population History*

[9] Shorters, 'Baswich', p. 14

[10] P. Rahtz, 'Wharram Percy memorial stones: an anthropological view from Mars', in ed. D Hooke, *Medieval Villages* (1985), pp. 214-223 (p. 219)

[11] *Ibid.* p. 219

[12] J. Harris, *Private Lives, Public Spirit: A Social History of Britain 1870-1914* (1993), pp. 50-54, cited hereafter as Harris, *Private Lives*

[13] E. Royle, *Modern Britain. A Social History 1750-1997* (1997), p. 48

[14] Porter, *Disease, Medicine and Society*, p. 62

[15] Victor Skipp, *The Making of Victorian Birmingham* (1983), pp. 87-88, cited hereafter as Skipp, *Victorian Birmingham*

[16] King's Norton had a railway station by 1850, and suburban railways developed in the 1870s for business people. Also aiding contact with Birmingham were tramways which spread out from the centre of Birmingham from the 1860s. For more details see Skipp, *Victorian Birmingham* and A. Briggs, *History of Birmingham. Volume II. Borough and City 1865-1938* (1952)

[17] Skipp, *Victorian Birmingham*, p. 64

[18] *Ibid.* p. 88

[19] Wrigley and Schofield, *Population History*, p. 476

[20] E. A. Wrigley, 'Family Reconstitution' in ed. E. A. Wrigley, *An Introduction to English Historical Demography: From the Sixteenth to the Nineteenth Century* (1966) p. 151

[21] P. Laslett, *The World We Have Lost: Further Explored* (1983), p. 112

[22] T. Molleson and M. Cox, *The Spitalfields Project. Volume 2: Anthropology*, Council For British Archaeology Research Report 86 (1993), p. 209, cited hereafter as Molleson and Cox, *Spitalfields 2*

[23] Louise Schewer, 'Age at Death and Cause of Death of the People Buried in St Bride's Church, Fleet Street, London', in ed. M. Cox, *Grave Concerns. Death and Burial in England 1700-1850*, Council for British Archaeology Research Report 118 (1998), pp. 100-112 (p. 101)

[24] Shorters, 'Baswich', p. 17

[25] December, January and February are classified as winter, March, April and May as spring, June, July and August as summer and September, October and November as autumn.

[26] Wrigley and Schofield, *Population History*, p. 293

[27] Shorters, 'Baswich', p. 21

[28] Wrigley and Schofield, *Population History*, p. 296

[29] *Ibid.* p. 305

[30] *Ibid.* p. 305

[31] Molleson and Cox, *Spitalfields 2*, p. 182

[32] D. E. C. Eversley, 'Exploitation of Anglican Parish Registers by Aggregative Analysis', in ed. E. A. Wrigley, *English Historical Demography: From the Sixteenth to the Nineteenth Century* (1966), p. 30

[33] Shorters, 'Baswich', p. 22

Chapter Two

SOCIO-ECONOMIC TRENDS AND SPATIAL ANALYSIS

Occupation

The inscriptions on the memorials were used to study the deceased's occupation. It does not appear to have been important to the people of King's Norton to record employment, as only 34 memorials out of 849 record it. At Wootton Wawen, a greater percentage of memorials record the occupation of the deceased; however, the figure was still statistically very small, only 21 out of 406.

At Wroxeter,[1] the occupation of the deceased was rarely given, except for a few incumbents of the church, schoolmasters, servants, and military men. The memorials at King's Norton show similar occupations. Thirteen memorials record occupations relating to the armed services, nine of the occupations recorded were related to the church and five to the law. Other occupations recorded were two surgeons, a headmaster and a teacher. On one memorial inside the church, occupation was important enough to warrant a lengthy description of the career of John Southern (MSA10), who worked with 'the celebrated establishment at Soho' applying his 'extensive knowledge of mathematics and physics to practical purposes'. Offices held, such as churchwardens and parish clerks, were also often recorded as a mark of social standing.

At Wootton Wawen religious occupations were again prominent, with seven vicars recorded. Five other people had occupations in the armed services, and two memorials list a Justice of the Peace and a magistrate. Other memorials recorded a nurse, a steward and a servant. Often, when servants were commemorated, the memorial stone was erected by their master. This is true in the case of MG43, erected by the family for whom the servant had worked for over 30 years.

The majority of occupations recorded at Wootton Wawen were, therefore, similar to those found at King's Norton. The remaining memorials recording occupation at Wootton Wawen show, more unusually, a blacksmith, a gunsmith, a paper maker, and a huntsman and farmer.

Where there is a high incidence of recording occupation, the results can be used in conjunction with time of year of death to analyse whether occupation played an important part in this. Unfortunately, the small number of occupations recorded at both King's Norton and Wootton Wawen mean that little more analysis can be done. A similar problem has been found in studies elsewhere. At Baswich,[2] only 15 memorials listed the employment of the deceased, and at Wharram Percy,[3] only three occupations were found on 31 stones. From these results it appears that the employment of the deceased was commonly not as important to record as the age of the person, date of death, lineage, and sentiment. When occupations are commemorated they are often used to emphasise the status of the deceased and what they had achieved in life.

First names and Place of origin

First names may hold good evidence of the outlook of a community and the influences they are subject to, so that when several yards are compared, they may show historically significant differences between them. Analysis may indicate the extent to which names are evidence of the outlook of communities and show how conservative or cosmopolitan they were. At both King's Norton and Wootton Wawen, the first names of the people recorded on the memorials were analysed to investigate what influenced their choice. Overall the results showed that in both churchyards biblical or other traditional names, such as those of English royalty and saints, were the most popular. Unfortunately little of value to the overall study was gained from this exercise because analysis of first names is not an exact science and it was difficult to categorise some of the names.

The memorials were analysed to investigate place of origin of the deceased as this could have shown evidence of immigration into the parish. However little could be gained from this exercise because so few people recorded place of origin at King's Norton (14.6 per cent) compared to Wootton Wawen (40 per cent). If a great deal more time had been available, combined use of the burial registers and the 1851 and later census lists would doubtless have shown much more about immigration into the parish.

Families

At King's Norton there were 570 different surnames. Forty-five percent of surnames are found only once and 68 per cent are found only once or twice, implying considerable mobility. The most frequently occurring surname is Smith (44 people), followed by Clulee (29), Pountney (25), and Greves (24). Several surnames occur for over a century, with a couple of family names predominating, such as the Lea family who are recorded between 1773 and 1888.

At Wootton Wawen there were 238 different surnames. Forty per cent of them are used only once, and 71 per cent are found only once or twice. The most frequently occurring surname is Hawkes with 23 people having this surname, followed by Smith (18), Cooper (16) and Hoitt (15). Several surnames occur for over a century such as Green, Tomes, Cooper and Smith. A couple of family names predominate, lasting for over a century, such as the Cooper family from 1796 to 1910. A greater number of family names occur for half a century, such as the Knight family from 1664 to 1727.

The inscriptions on the memorials at King's Norton were used to investigate kinship. The largest number of people commemorated on one stone is 31 (MD847). They are recorded on a chest tomb belonging to the Pountney family. Twenty-one people are commemorated on a memorial attached to one of the church's external faces. This belongs to the Greves family (MF723). The most frequently occurring number of people recorded on one stone is two: 36.9 per cent of the stones commemorate two people, 19 per cent of the stones commemorate only one person. A large number of stones commemorate more than two people on them with 17.6 per cent of the stones commemorating three people and 12.8 per cent of stones commemorating four or more people on them. Marital relationships appear to be important to record, with 326 out of 784 memorials (42 per cent) indicating a marital relationship compared to 100 out of 784 (12.7 per cent) referring to a familial relationship. Twenty-six per cent of stones refer to both, but 19.4 per cent of the stones refer to neither relationship. At King's Norton, it appears to be important for married women to be buried with their husband. Few women were commemorated alone; most followed their husband's family in death but 30 women were buried with their parental family. Occasionally family ties are very strong, such as in the case of Cordelia Southern (formerly Dobbs), her husband and their children, who were living in Handsworth but came to King's Norton to be buried in her father's tomb inside the church. Several stones indicate that people were married more than once, with three stones commemorating the husband and both first and second wives, and one stone commemorating a woman and both her first and her second husband.

The inscriptions on the memorials at Wootton Wawen were also used to investigate families. The largest number of people recorded on a memorial is eight, on a headstone commemorating the Horsley family (MB56). The most frequently occurring number of people on a memorial is one (51 per cent), followed by two (33 per cent). Only sixteen percent of stones commemorate more than two people. Marital relationships appear to be important to record with 124 out of 362 memorials (34 per cent) indicating a marital relationship compared with 52 (14.4 per cent) recording a familial relationship. Sixty-six memorials indicate both (18.2 per cent). Most people thought that it was important to record lineage as only 33 per cent of the memorials do not indicate either relationship. It appears to be particularly important at Wootton Wawen for married women to be buried with their husband and his family as only five are recorded as being buried with their parents. Few married women are commemorated alone and on several of those memorials it appears that space was left at the top of the memorial to commemorate the husband. Two women who had moved away came back to be buried with family, and several stones indicate that people were married more than once. On three stones both wives are commemorated together, one of whom had remarried after her first husband died.

The memorials were analysed to estimate the size of families. At King's Norton 28 per cent of the memorials could be used for this. The largest number of children recorded was eight, on a memorial commemorating the Bates family. On the memorial stones where children were recorded the results indicate that most families had

one child (66.5 per cent) with 20.9 per cent having two and 7.1 per cent having three. Only 5.9 per cent of the memorials indicated four or more children.

At Wootton Wawen 18.4 per cent of stones could be used to estimate the size of families. The largest number of children recorded was 16 on the Somervile memorial in the church (MSC3). Only nine of the children survived their father. On the Barran memorial (MA12), 12 children were recorded, eight of whom were dead before their parents. The most frequently recorded number of children found was one (43 per cent), followed by two (29.8 per cent). Only 15.5 per cent of families recorded more than three children. The results of analysing the size of families agree with those found at Baswich,[4] where most families had only one child.

The analysis of the memorial inscriptions has provided some information about family sizes. It is, however, extremely difficult to estimate family sizes from memorial stones. The number of memorials that can be used to analyse this is low and so the analysis is hampered, and the results are also potentially inaccurate because of the probable lack of commemoration of children. As marital links appear to be more important to record, links between parents and children may be missed. Another problem is that older children may have moved from the area, or female children may have married and not have had their maiden name recorded. At King's Norton only 16 maiden names were found, and at Wootton Wawen 11. No one else doing similar work has tried this and so there is not a lot of comparative material available. It is important, therefore, to test the data as much as possible to see how the information gained from the memorials is historically useful and reliable when investigating families.

Spatial analysis

The plan of the churchyard[5] was used for a spatial analysis of the graves at King's Norton (Figure 20). Investigations elsewhere have found that the exact alignment of graves varies considerably as they are affected by the nearest dominant topographical feature.[6] At Wroxeter,[7] it was found that graves close to the church and those near to the north boundary of the churchyard were affected by these features, and those near to the road were at right angles to it. The alignment of graves at King's Norton was measured with a compass, and this produced some interesting results. All of the burials initially look to be strictly aligned west-east (to judge from the positions of the memorials). This is in accordance with the customary mode of burial, which is thought to have its origins in primitive sun worship.[8] There are, however, differences of up to 30° between some graves in one area. Least affected are those furthest north in the churchyard. There has been much clearance in this area but the remaining graves are all aligned true west-east. Burials around the church follow the alignment of the church and those furthest west of the church appear to have been affected by the pathway leading to the Vicarage. Graves in section H, to the east and south-east of the church, appear to be most affected by the pathway.

Some are aligned up to 30° south of true west-east. The boundary next to the main road affects the graves closest to it which vary between 10° north and 40° south of true west-east. The alignment of the burials in section G appears to be affected less by the pathway than by the need for space. This is because this area, close to the church door and on the main pathway to the church, was very popular for burial. In this section there is no specific emphasis on west-east burial with the graves being aligned to make the best possible use of space. Similar results were found during an investigation at Spitalfields where alignment was dictated by space when a west-east position was not found.[9]

The results from Wootton Wawen are similar. Figure 21 shows clearly that the alignment of the burials was affected by contiguous features. Graves were clearly affected by pathways in all areas of the churchyard, particularly the main entrance to the church, where the graves are aligned up to 30° south of true west-east for visibility. Memorials in the north of the churchyard were affected by the pathway running through the yard and those in sections B and C were affected by the main boundary to the west and by the pathway that runs through this area. The newest burials placed there in recent years follow the trend of the earlier ones and are aligned at 20° south of true west-east. Burials by the church doors differ in alignment from those beyond them and are again aligned for visibility.

Geography of the yard

The plan of the churchyard was used to look at how its geography developed over time (Figure 22). At King's Norton the earliest memorials, dated between 1700 and 1799, are all found in the area closest to the church, and areas to the south and east of the church. The most popular areas for burial in churchyards are generally the south and east sides of the church, particularly the south side which is most often in the public view. The east is thought of as the home of sunrise and hope, and the south is home of the warmth of midday and is most often in the public view because of the southern doorway of the church.[10] Memorials dated between 1800 and 1849 are found in the areas surrounding the church in the south, east and west, while those of 1850-1899 are again found around the church and also extend to the north. The north side of the church is traditionally less popular because of prejudice rooted in folk beliefs. It was seen as vulnerable to witchcraft and the devil, and was often used for burial of suicides, criminals, paupers, strangers and the unbaptized, until limitations of space meant that it was necessary to use this for burial.[11] Memorials dated between 1900 and 1940 are again found in sections J to K to the north of the church, and then in the extensions to the west side of the churchyard. The partial clearance of the north side of the churchyard has left wide gaps of space which are now being filled again. The cleared stones have been mainly used to form a pathway through sections J to L, around the church, and to build a small wall around section E. There has also been some infilling throughout the churchyard and very modern stones are to be found in all areas.

At King's Norton only 14.3 per cent of memorials had the place of origin on them. These few memorials indicate that the place of origin was not an important factor in the development of the geography of the churchyard at King's Norton. There does not appear to be any tendency for people from the various civil parishes or townships to cluster in specific parts of the yard.

Place of origin was not important in the development of the churchyard but the geography does appear to have been heavily influenced by kin grouping (Figure 19). Several families are represented on more than one memorial. The importance of being buried with family is indicated by what appear to be several family plots. These were mostly of only two graves, but there are several family groups of three or four memorials. The Lea/Oakes family has the largest group of memorials, with three plaques and two memorials along the north side of the church. The Pountney family have four memorials, all in the area directly opposite the west door of the church. The Gem family have three memorials around the entrances to the south door and the west door. There may be other family groups or members of families who have not been identified. It is difficult to be totally accurate because some people may be linked even though there is no clear indication of this on the memorials. Illegible stones may also contain further family links. Despite this problem the results show a significant family influence on the development of the graveyard. Finding family groups on such a large scale indicates that people felt that it was important to be together in death as in life.

The plan of Wootton Wawen churchyard was used to look at how the geography of the churchyard developed over time (Figure 23). The earliest memorials (1700 to 1749) are found in areas closest to the church, with a group of nine of them by the north door. Memorials of 1750 to 1799 are again found around the church, but also extend further north. Memorials dated 1800 to 1849 are dotted around the churchyard, as are memorials from 1850 to 1899, when there is a larger concentration in the very north of the yard. The largest concentration of memorials from 1900 to 1940 is found in section B and C in the twentieth century extension and there has also been some infilling in all areas of the churchyard.

The earliest Henley memorials are found in section B, where no other places of origin are recorded. As time goes on it appears that place of origin is less important in the development of the geography of the churchyard. It is possible that there was another grouping of Henley memorials between 1850 and 1899 in section E. Other groupings of Henley-in-Arden memorials are related to family plots. Family groups are very important in the development of the churchyard (Figure 26). They are found throughout the yard, except in the extension. Most are of groups of two memorials. There are two groups of six memorials, one to the Hoitt family in section F and the other to the Smith family in section D in the northernmost part of the churchyard. The Hawkes family has a group of eight memorials in section E. The largest group of memorials is twelve. This group is in section G, and commemorates members of the Cooper family.

Burial inside the church

There was a strong desire to be placed in death as close to a source of spiritual power as possible,[12] and a desire to show social status. It was considered important to maintain standards of class in death, as in life, and if possible to use death as a means of social advancement.[13] In the medieval period and for a considerable period thereafter only the most important people were buried inside a church; and so to be buried there was an indication of considerable status, being originally limited to ecclesiastics, benefactors of the church and those of royal birth. By the eighteenth century it was often reserved for people of high status and wealth. It was frowned upon by ecclesiastical authorities but by the mid-eighteenth century even minor gentry often managed to find their way in.[14] The church was often put to excessive use for intramural burial. Some families even 'reserved' space inside the church.[15]

Research at Baswich showed that it was particularly difficult to be buried or commemorated inside the church. Over the whole period from 1587 to 1900, apart from the memorials of two families and their servants, there are only three other memorials inside the church. Although burial in the church does not appear to be as exclusive at King's Norton and Wootton Wawen as at Baswich, the location of memorials inside it appears to have been strongly influenced by kin grouping and status. It was considered particularly important to commemorate family members on memorials even if they were buried in the churchyard outside or further afield. In the mid-nineteenth century legislation brought intramural burial to an end, owing to alleged public health dangers, but people continued to put up memorials to commemorate family members whenever they could. From the memorials inside both churches it also appears to have been important to record any estates and houses in possession of the family. High status is shown on the memorials in the church, with many having heraldry on them and recording a title, such as esquire, as part of the inscription.

At Wootton Wawen there are 57 memorials inside the church, recording 64 people. Thirty-five of these memorials commemorate 43 people from only four families (Figure 24). Most of the memorials record only one person. There are 14 memorials in the chancel, 11 memorials in the nave and 32 in the south chapel. Memorials inside the church show the importance of kinship, property and titles in obtaining commemoration there.

Several of the prominent family groups were buried inside the church because the estates they owned gave them that right. The owners and proprietors of the manor of Wootton had burial rights on the north side of the chapel and the owners of the manor of Edstone had rights and responsibilities on its south side.[16] This meant that the lords, their families and people connected intimately with them are recorded inside the church. A good example of the type of people buried there for this reason is the Somervile family.[17] Their ownership of the manor and estates of Edstone (in the parish of Wootton Wawen)

began in the reign of Edward IV when Thomas Somervile, a member of the ancient family of Aston Somervile in Gloucestershire, married the daughter of John Aylesbury, the lord of Edstone.[18] The earliest memorial found to a Somervile is SC3 on the south wall in the chapel which records William Somervile of Edstone, esquire (died 1676). He married Ann, daughter of John, Viscount Tracy, and had 11 sons (six of whom survived him) and five daughters (three survived him). His status is indicated by the arms of his family at the top of the memorial.

His estate passed to his eldest son Robert, esquire, who died in 1705 and is commemorated next to his father on the south wall (SC4) and has a flat stone recording his actual place of burial (SC 25). He married Elizabeth, daughter of Sir Charles Wolsely of Wolsely, and had seven children. His fifth son, Reverend Edward Somervile (died 1734), is commemorated on the same memorial and also has a marker stone for his burial in the chapel (SC 31). Elizabeth died in 1742 and is commemorated on SC29 amongst the flat stones of the family. The estate then passed to his eldest son William Somervile, esquire, who is described on N8 as 'the poet of the chace.' His wife Mary died in 1731 and is commemorated on SC21 in the south chapel. William died in July 1742 and was buried in the chapel at Wootton under a flat stone (SC20) just to the north of his wife's. On three of the Somervile memorials are the family arms.

Other families who are buried in the church because of the rights they had as owners of the manor of Edstone are the Knight family and the Phillips family. The Smith/Harewell/Carington family are an example of a family, many of whom were Catholic, who were buried in the parish church because of their rights as owners of the manor of Wootton. Close to the memorials of this family on the north side of the chapel is the memorial to Reverend Father Frost who may have been chaplain to the Smith/Harewell/Carington family at Wootton Hall where there was a small Roman Catholic chapel at the house. His connection with an important family may have been the reason for his burial inside the parish church. These families are discussed in more detail in Appendix 1.

Other people who were buried inside the church were vicars and curates of the parish. There are three memorials there to vicars. Twelve others indicate that the people commemorated on them were buried inside the church but it is difficult to tell why. Many appear to have no other links inside the church or with memorials in the churchyard. Five of the memorials show status by referring to titles such as esquire, Mr or gent. One memorial to a Roman Catholic shows status with the use of heraldry.

Where there is no direct reference to burial inside the church in the inscription it can be difficult to tell whether people were buried there or only commemorated. An example of this is the memorials to the Galton family. The Galtons, who were connected with the Phillips family who are buried inside, have a large vault outside in the churchyard next to the south wall of the church, to which their memorials are fixed. This may act as the entrance to a vault underneath the church.

During the period when intramural burial was still permitted there were many people who were only commemorated inside the church but not actually buried there. These were connected with families buried inside the church. An example is four of the memorials to the Knight family.[19] As owner of the sub-manor of Barrels, Robert Knight had tried to claim rights to burial inside the church.[20] His claim was not allowed and shows that wealth was not the overriding factor in obtaining burial here. The manor of Edstone was purchased by Robert Knight, in 1745 which finally brought him rights in the chapel. As well as memorials to those of his family who were buried inside the church Robert Knight, who became Earl of Catherlough from 1763, erected them to others, including his sisters, parents and grandparents, who had died before he had rights in the chapel and had been buried elsewhere. This shows his pride and concern for his family in which an established burial place played no little part.

Since an Order in Council of 1882 forbade any further interments in the church,[21] only seven memorials have been placed inside it. It does not appear to have been much easier to get commemoration at this time as the types of people found are very similar to those who had obtained burial and commemoration earlier.

Important people with estates in the parish who would perhaps have previously been buried inside the church were now merely commemorated. George Henry Capewell Hughes, esquire, bought Wootton Hall in 1904. He has a large tomb in the churchyard but shows his status in the church with a tablet displaying heraldry, which records his death in 1906. Other memorials commemorating people associated with those of high status are SA2 and MN5, which are connected with the Somervile family. SA2 commemorates John Hoitt, huntsman to William Somervile, and is a copy of the churchyard original. This memorial was erected in 1902, on the centenary of Hoitt's death. N5 was erected in 1898 to commemorate William Somervile. Other people who continued to be commemorated were vicars such as Reverend Francis Thomas Bramston who died in 1916.

It is difficult to tell why some people were commemorated inside the church. George Clark, a builder, and his wife are actually buried in the very north of the churchyard. They are commemorated inside the nave but show no connection with other people inside the church, or connections with any of the manors. It is possible that they were benefactors of the church.

Despite the exclusion of many people from burial inside the church, other families of high status used the location of their memorials and their size to indicate their social position. For families who could not quite get burial inside the church, a pedestal tomb or chest tomb was often the perfect choice to show superiority.[22] Outside in the churchyard families who were recorded on memorials inside the church but not actually buried there are found in the most prominent locations. Because there are only a few large memorials at Wootton Wawen, they are very prominent. One of these is the Galton vault (MA13). This is a very large monument in the best position on the pathway leading to the main door.

The types of people buried inside the church was analysed at King's Norton. There are 48 memorials inside the church, commemorating 167 people. Twenty-six of these memorials commemorate 72 people from only seven families (Figure 25). Only six memorials are now in the chancel, which, as it contains the high altar was therefore 'close to God,' and was the preferred location for burial inside the church.[23] The nave, giving lesser spiritual benefit, was cheaper. Most of the memorials at King's Norton were located in the north and south aisle.

With many more people buried inside the church than at Wootton Wawen, trying to analyse the types of people buried inside the church at King's Norton was less clearcut. As at Wootton Wawen several of the families buried inside the church were the lords of the manors of King's Norton. A good example is the Taylor family who have two memorials in the church. These suggest the importance of those recorded by describing their abode as Moseley Hall and by the use of the titles esquire and 'Lord of this manor'. The Taylor family were the principal landowners in Moseley. They are an example of the new gentry whose wealth was founded on industry. The manor of Moseley was purchased in 1767 by John Taylor of Bordesley Park.[24] He was a button and snuff box manufacturer and in 1765, with his son John, was cofounder with Sampson Lloyd of Lloyds Bank.[25] His son inherited the estate in 1775. He is commemorated on memorial SA24. Moseley Hall stayed in the Taylor family until 1852 when James Taylor died. He is commemorated on MNA10. Having bought the rights to the manor of King's Norton in 1804 John was important enough to be buried inside the church in a vault under the vestry. Another family who were buried inside the church because of their manorial connections were the Middlemore family. John Middlemore, died in 1698 and is recorded on MSA7 as a 'descendant of the antient family of Middlemores, former Lords of the manor of Edgbaston, Studley and Hazlewell halls'.

Other families who were buried inside the church were owners of smaller estates in King's Norton parish. An example of these is the Dobbs family. They have six memorials in the south aisle. There is no heraldry on these memorials but the importance of the family is indicated in the inscription, which shows that they are from Lifford Hall. The memorials in the church commemorate Thomas and Cordelia Dobbs and their children and grandchildren who died between 1803 and 1873. Their eldest daughter and her husband, John Southern of Oakhill in Handsworth (who is described in his inscription as 'distinguished by his acquaintance with mathematics and physical science'), were buried with other members of the Dobbs family in the family vault inside the church. Other people who were buried inside the church and were owners of smaller estates in the parish are William Hicks, and the Pountney family of Monyhull Hall. Another memorial shows that landholding was also important. Memorial SA16 commemorates Sarah East who died in 1725. Sarah was the wife of Henry East of Sladepool, a wealthy landowner. Henry was buried amongst his ancestors inside the church at Yardley. The memorial tablet contains six shields displaying the family arms.

Another family with vaults under the church was the Gem family. They were possibly not members of the gentry, with few references to titles and no heraldry on their memorials, but gained burial inside the church through their personal and financial status. They list their abodes as Brandwood House and Hazlewell Hall. Many of them were attorneys and owned Brandwood House in King's Heath for over a century.

Three other memorials to people who were buried inside the church commemorate vicars of the parish, including Reverend James Hemming who died in 1767. Family connections with the vicar may also have been the reason for people from the Whitehouse/Lyttelton family being buried in the church. There is no heraldry on the memorials and no titles.

Several of the people buried inside the church have no references to estates and indicate no links with other families inside the church. The memorials are to George Burrish, esquire, of Birmingham, Elizabeth Laugher and John Reeve, gent. It is difficult to tell why they were buried there. They were possibly benefactors of the church.

Several of the memorials inside the church record people who were not buried there, only commemorated. It appears to have been difficult even to get commemorated inside the church, with the same types of people being commemorated as were buried. Two memorials were to people whose family were buried inside but they were buried elsewhere, such as Roger Truslove Gem who was buried at Highgate Cemetery in London but is commemorated inside with his family on memorial C8.

Four memorials commemorate people who were buried in the churchyard, being for members of the Whitehouse family buried outside the church in a family vault but connected with people buried inside it. The entrance of the vault is inscribed, but otherwise there is only a plain stone bearing the inscription 'Mr W D Whitehouse's (of Studley) vault'.

The three other memorials were to members of the Lane family who had manorial connections. There is a small shield on one of the memorials. They record Sarah and Joseph Lane, Thomas and Anne Lane of Moundsley Hall, and two of their daughters. The Lane family owned Moundsley from 1852 until 1936.[26]

It was still difficult to get commemoration inside the church after the end of intramural burial. Four of the memorials commemorate people who were connected with the church. Two were vicars and two were churchwardens. Three memorials commemorate people of the parish who had died during warfare. Three other memorials commemorate people who have family members buried inside the church. These relate to members of the Gem and the Whitehouse families who died after intramural burial was prohibited.

Status and ownership of estates helped to gain commemoration inside the church. Another of the important houses in King's Norton was The Priory, King's Heath. One of the owners, John Cartland, a Justice of the Peace for the County, and his wife Ann are recorded on memorial NA7 on the north wall of the church, with a small shield displaying heraldry. Their death in the late nineteenth century meant that they were buried outside in the churchyard.

For eight of the memorials inside the church it is difficult to tell whether the people were buried inside or just commemorated. Two to members of the Dobbs family and one to Joseph Rann gent, are partly illegible. The two memorials to the Mynors family who died between 1797 and 1842 give no indication of where they were buried. The inscription shows that they were the owners of Weatheroak Hall in Moseley, which remained in the family's ownership until 1936. They also held the manor of Kingsuch.[27] Their status is emphasised with the use of 'esquire' in the inscription, and in the lengthy description recording that Robert Mynors was a surgeon. The memorial to the Reverend Joseph Amphlett (MC6) also gives no indication of whether he was buried inside the church.

The final two memorials record members of the Pountney family. It is difficult to tell which of the family were buried inside the church because although one of the memorials indicates a family vault under the vestry, all of the Pountney family commemorated inside the church are also recorded on the family tomb outside.

The next best thing to being buried inside the church was to be buried in the churchyard as close as possible. In many of the best positions at King's Norton are again those with ancestors buried inside the church. The huge pedestal tomb commemorating other members of the Middlemore family (ME535) is difficult to miss because of its imposing position close to the lychgate, which serves as the entrance to the churchyard. An excellent position to be seen by many people was as near to the west door as possible. Here the Pountney family have a large chest tomb opposite the west door commemorating 31 people, which even now takes the eye away from all of the memorials surrounding it (MD847). Another good place to be in the eyes of passers-by was by the south doorway. Here the Gem family have a large tomb opposite the entrance (ME521), and the Brettle/Greves/Palmer family have an enormous tablet fixed to the exterior of the church wall (MF723). Situated outside the main church door, it would be hard not to notice this expression of status. Another favoured place in the churchyard was the ground behind the east wall as it is close to the altar.[28] Here the Lea/Oakes family have their memorials as close as possible with a large chest tomb and several tablets fixed to the exterior wall.

In the minds of the living these areas were the second best locations for securing commemoration.[29] Other families drew attention to themselves by having their stones in prominent positions along the pathways to the church. To the north of the churchyard in view of the main pathway the Lane family (commemorated inside the church) have a large memorial over a vault (MI800), which has been added to by more recent family memorials. Also in this area is the Cartland memorial (MI804), a large pedestal tomb for the JP who was recorded on a memorial inside the church. Also in this area standing north of the vestry is a large pedestal tomb to William Hamper, esquire (MI806). William Hamper was a Fellow of the Society of Antiquaries and a Justice of the Peace.

The late nineteenth century brings the end for intramural burial but the emphasis on status does not end. The twentieth century saw large-scale monuments generally going out of fashion, but for some people size was still important. As the land directly around the church was full up families looked to the land to the north of the churchyard to build their enormous tombs and obelisks. Eleven large tombs and four enormous monuments still stand prominently in this area, as after clearance the more modern memorials found here are small plaques and curb stones. Even in the midst of uniform rows of curbs in the extension to the west of the church there is a chance to try to show status. Memorial B30, an extremely imposing one, records Henry Michael Grant (died 1926) and his wife Rosa (died 1938). It might not be on a main pathway but showing these people's status has been achieved because the monument can be seen easily from far away.

When trying to analyse the types of people buried inside the church it is important to remember that the surviving memorials represent only a tiny fraction of the actual number of burials that occurred in most churches.[30] Even though this is the case they can often give a good indication of the sorts of people who managed to be buried there. The results at both Wootton Wawen and King's Norton show that it was very largely the traditional landowning families of the parish, benefactors of the church and professional people.

[1] P. A. Rahtz, 'Wroxeter Churchyard 1974', *West Midlands Archaeological News Sheet*, 17 (1974), pp. 28-31 (p. 31) cited hereafter as Rahtz, 'Wroxeter'
[2] I. Shorters, 'A study of the grave memorials of Holy Trinity Church, Baswich, Staffordshire' (University of Birmingham, unpublished BA dissertation, 2000), p. 31, cited hereafter as Shorters, 'Baswich'
[3] P. A. Rahtz, 'Wharram Percy: an anthropological view from Mars', in ed. D. Hooke, *Medieval Villages* (1985), pp. 214-223 (p. 219), cited hereafter as Rahtz, 'Wharram Percy'
[4] Shorters, 'Baswich', p. 25
[5] The plans of the churchyards have been reduced for the dimensions of the publication and so some of the record numbers of the memorial stones may be illegible.
[6] W. Rodwell, *The Archaeology of the English Church* (1981), p. 132, cited hereafter as Rodwell, *Archaeology*
[7] Rahtz, 'Wroxeter', p. 28
[8] F. Burgess, *English Churchyard Memorials* (1963), p. 26, cited hereafter as Burgess, *Memorials*
[9] T. Molleson and M. Cox, *The Spitalfields Project. Volume 2: Anthropology*, Council For British Archaeology Research Report 86 (1993), p. 199
[10] W. Johnson, *Byways in British Archaeology* (1912), pp. 328-330
[11] Burgess, *Memorials*, p. 25
[12] J. Reeve and M. Adams, *The Spitalfields Project. Volume 1: The Archaeology*, Council for British Archaeology Research Report 85 (1993), p. 65
[13] J. Morley, *Death, Heaven and the Victorians* (London, 1971), p. 11
[14] ed. D J Steel, *National Index of Parish Registers. Volume 1. Sources of Births, Marriages and Deaths before 1837* (1968), p. 246
[15] J. Litten, *The English Way of Death. The Common Funeral Since 1450* (1991), p. 199, cited hereafter as Litten, *Death*
[16] William Cooper, *Wootton Wawen: Its History and Records* (1936), pp. 91-92, cited hereafter as Cooper, *Wootton Wawen*
[17] *Ibid.* pp. 67-73
[18] ed. L. F. Salzman, The Victoria History of the Counties of England, *Warwickshire, Volume III, Barlichway Hundred* (1945), pp. 199-200
[19] More detail about the Knight family is given in Appendix 1
[20] Cooper, *Wootton Wawen*, pp. 62-66 (p. 64)
[21] *Ibid.* p. 94
[22] B. Bailey, *Churchyards of England and Wales* (1987), p. 125
[23] Litten, *Death*, p. 200
[24] ed. J. W. Willis-Bund, The Victoria History of the Counties of England, *Worcestershire, Volume III* (1913), p. 185, cited hereafter as VCH, *Worcs*, III
[25] H. Goodger, *King's Norton* (1990), p. 17
[26] VCH, *Worcs* III, pp. 185-186
[27] *Ibid.* pp. 185-186
[28] K. Lindley, *Of Graves and Epitaphs* (1965), p. 86
[29] Rahtz, 'Wharram Percy', p. 216
[30] Rodwell, *Archaeology*, p. 146

Figure 19. King's Norton; plan of the churchyard showing possible family groups

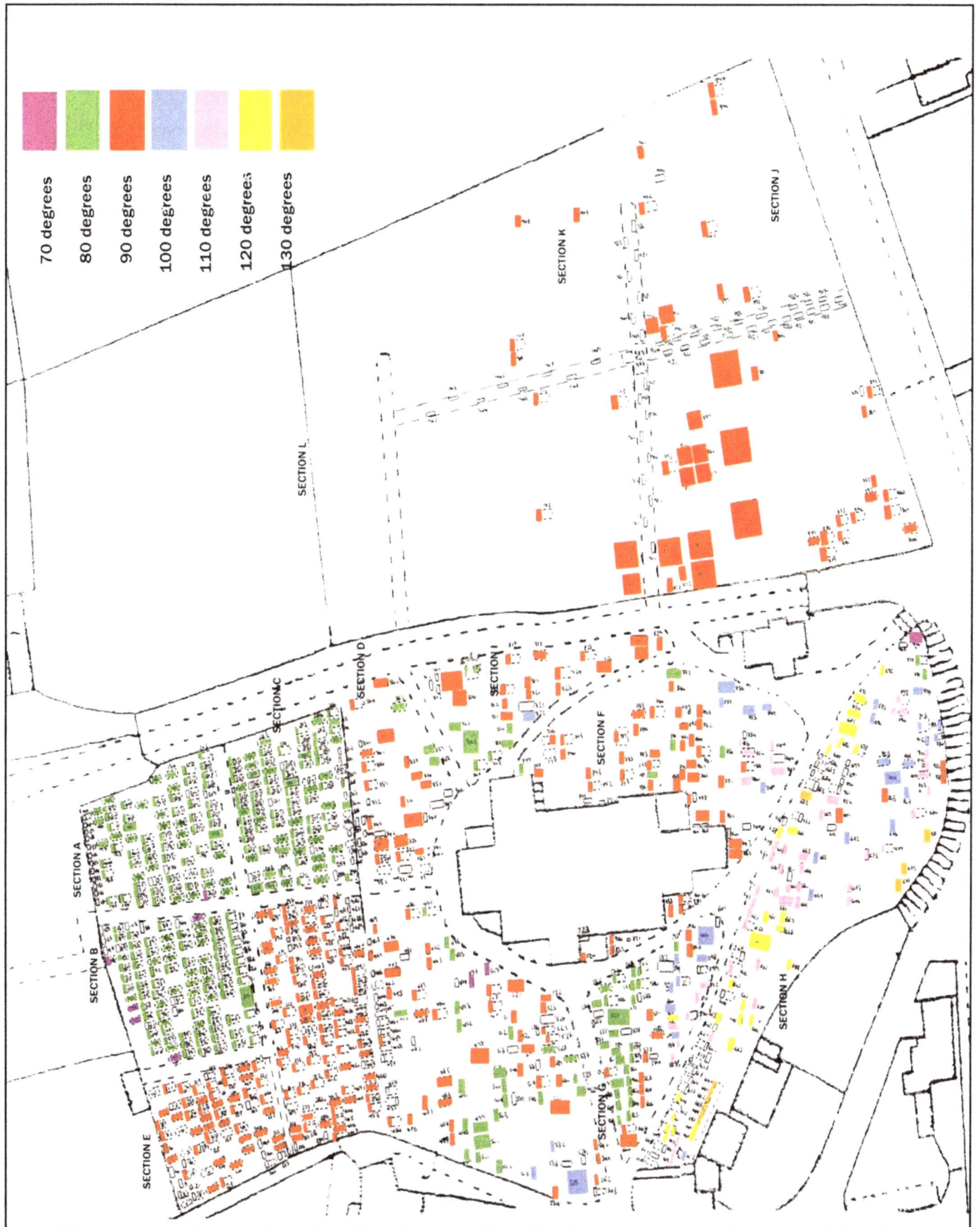

Figure 20. King's Norton: plan of the churchyard showing the alignment of the memorials

Legend:
- 70 degrees
- 80 degrees
- 90 degrees
- 100 degrees
- 110 degrees
- 120 degrees
- 130 degrees

SECTION A
SECTION B
SECTION C
SECTION D
SECTION E
SECTION F
SECTION G
SECTION H
SECTION I
SECTION J
SECTION K
SECTION L

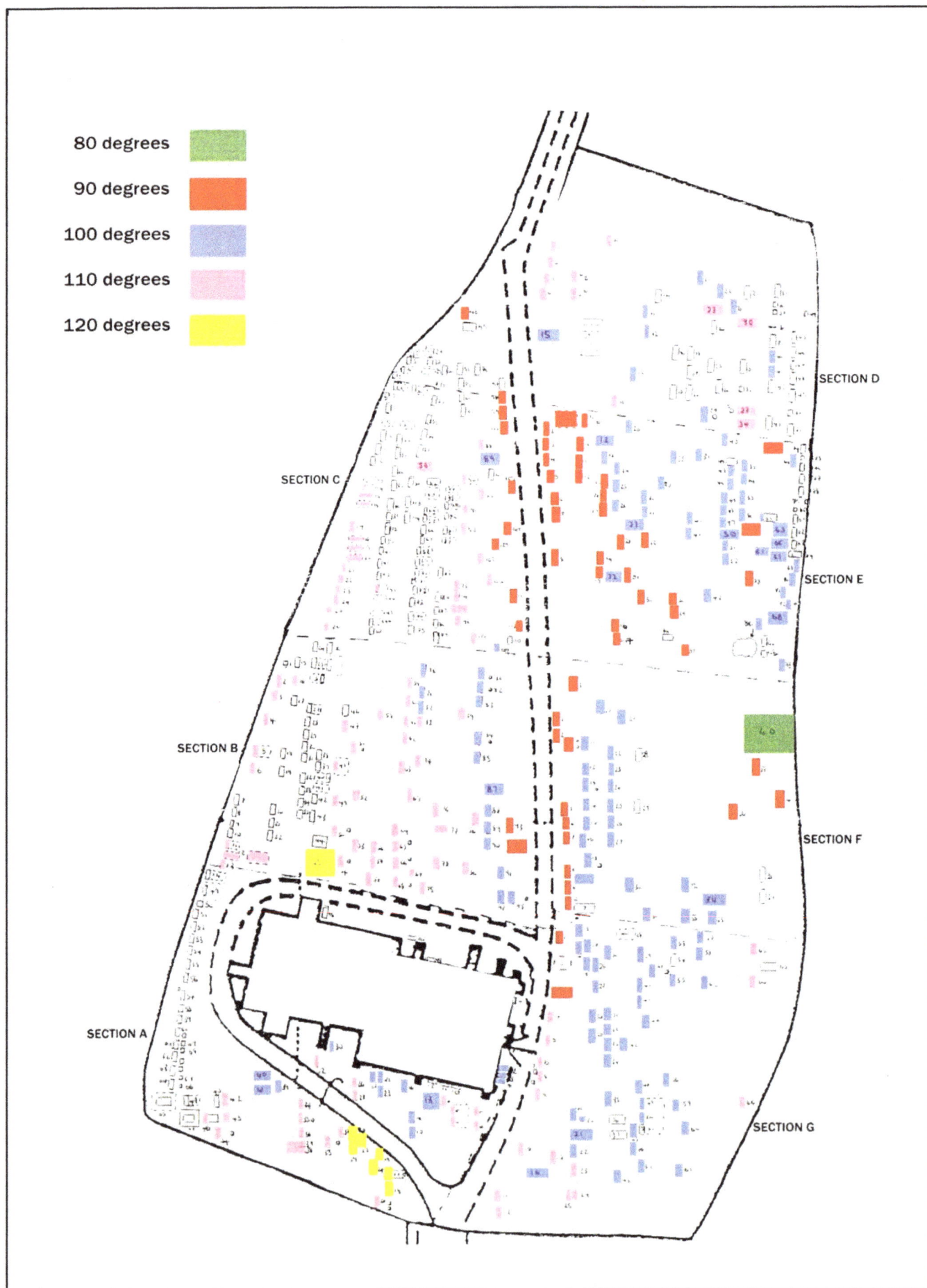

Figure 21. Wootton Wawen: plan of the churchyard showing the alignment of the memorials

Figure 22. King's Norton: plan of the churchyard showing the location of memorials over time

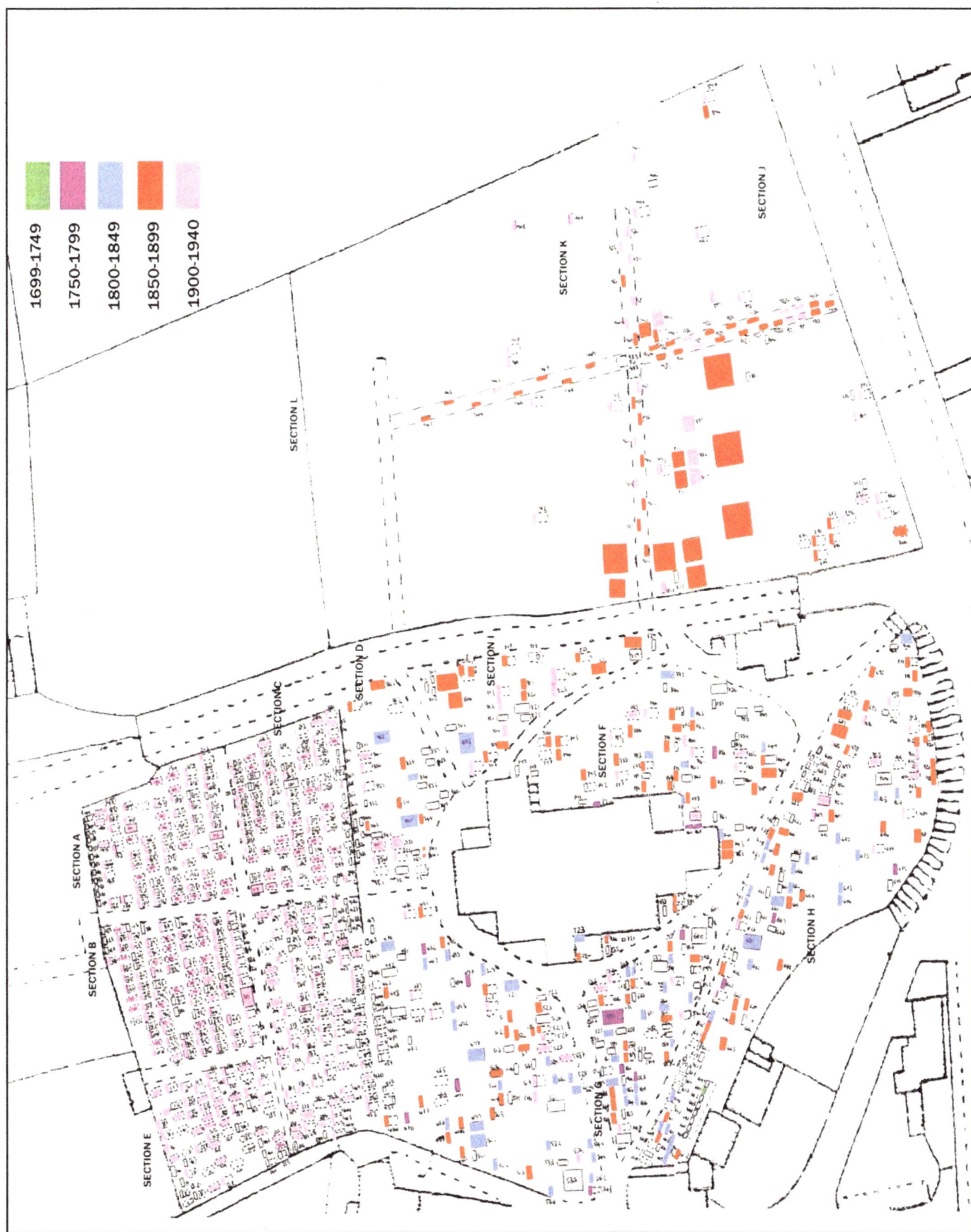

Figure 23. Wootton Wawen: plan of the churchyard showing the location of memorials over time

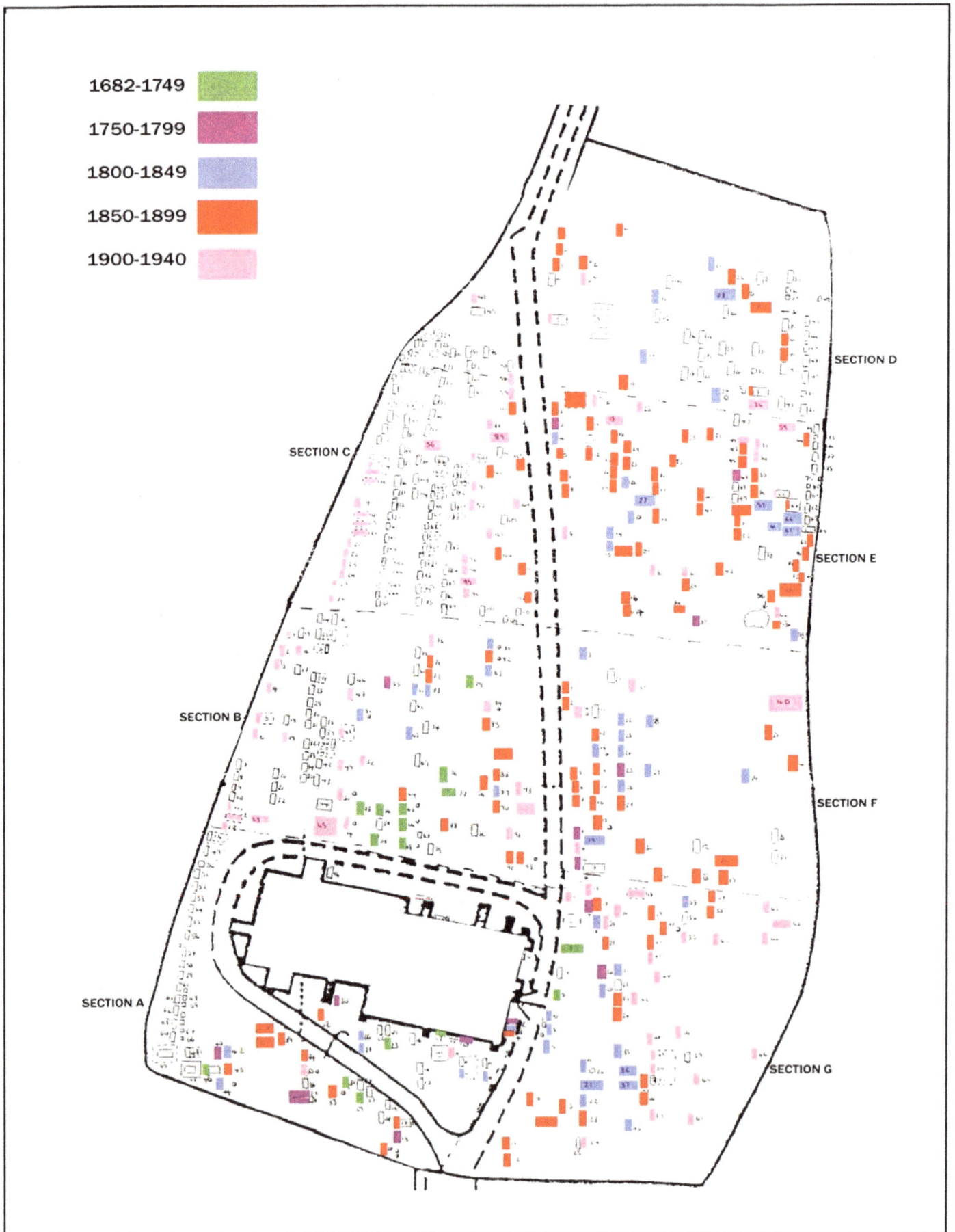

1682-1749

1750-1799

1800-1849

1850-1899

1900-1940

SECTION D

SECTION C

SECTION E

SECTION B

SECTION F

SECTION A

SECTION G

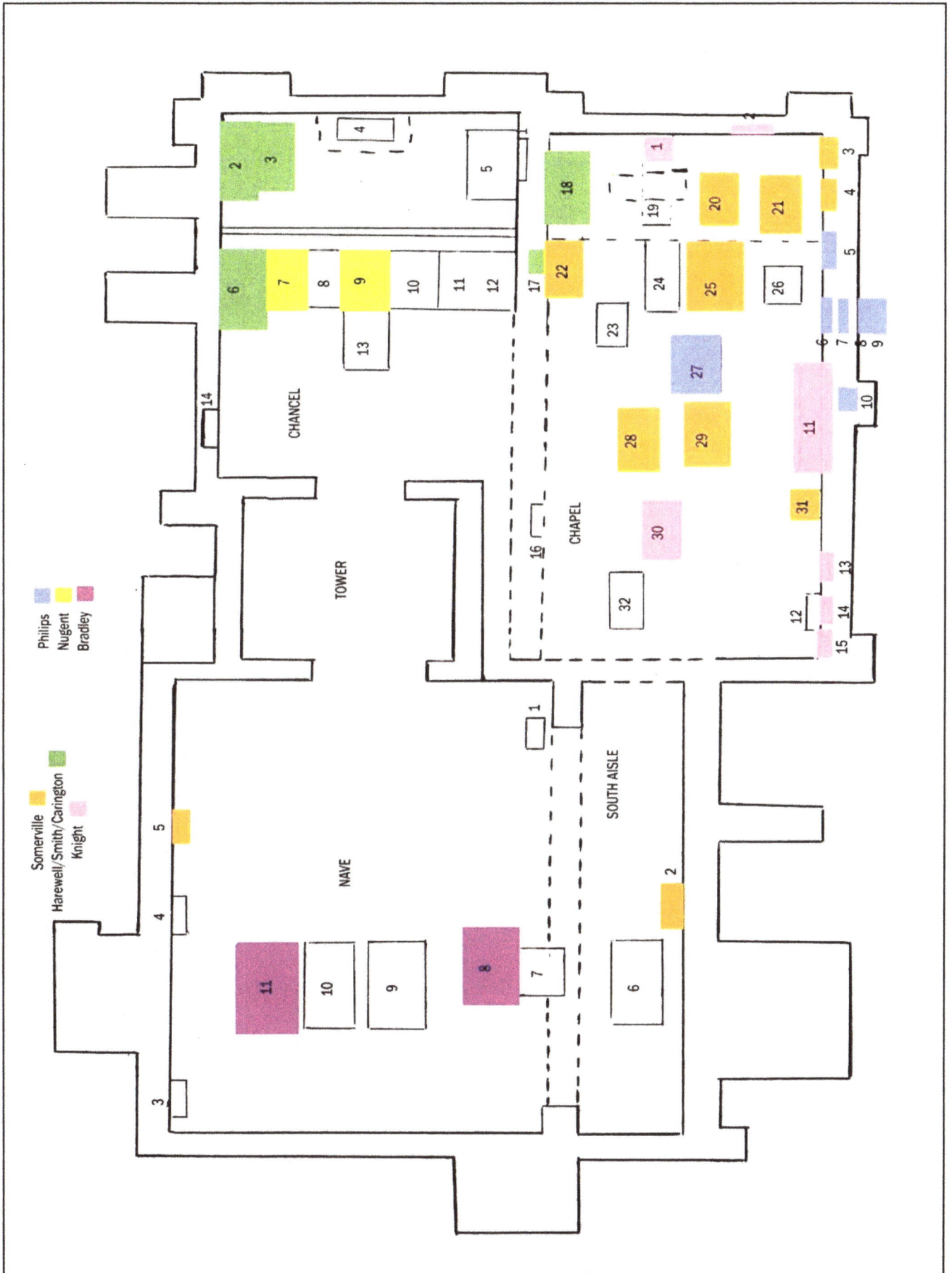

Figure 24. Wootton Wawen: plan of inside the church showing family groups

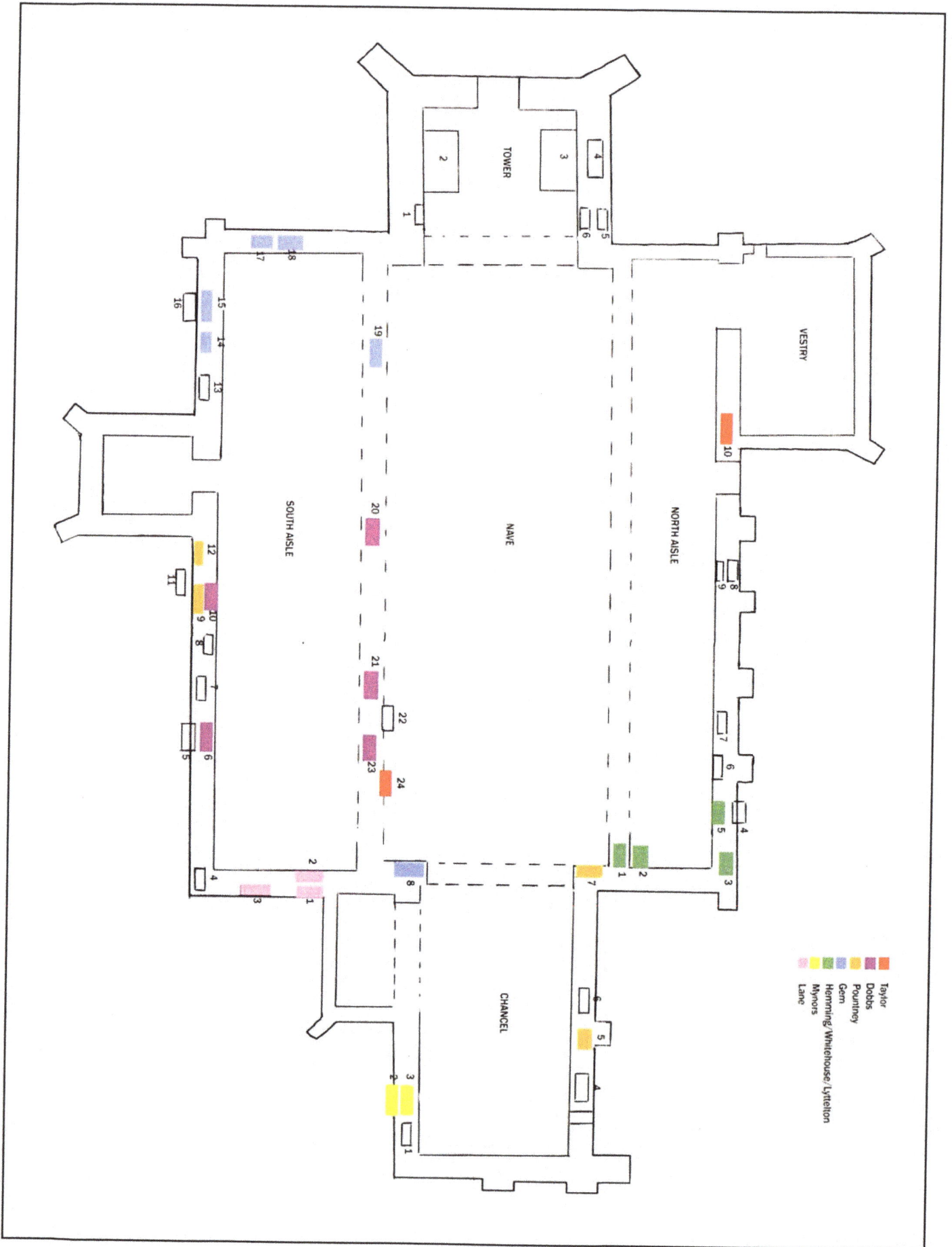

Figure 25. King's Norton: plan of inside the church showing family groups

TOWER

VESTRY

NAVE

NORTH AISLE

SOUTH AISLE

CHANCEL

Taylor
Dobbs
Pountney
Gem
Hemming/Whitehouse/Lyttelton
Mynors
Lane

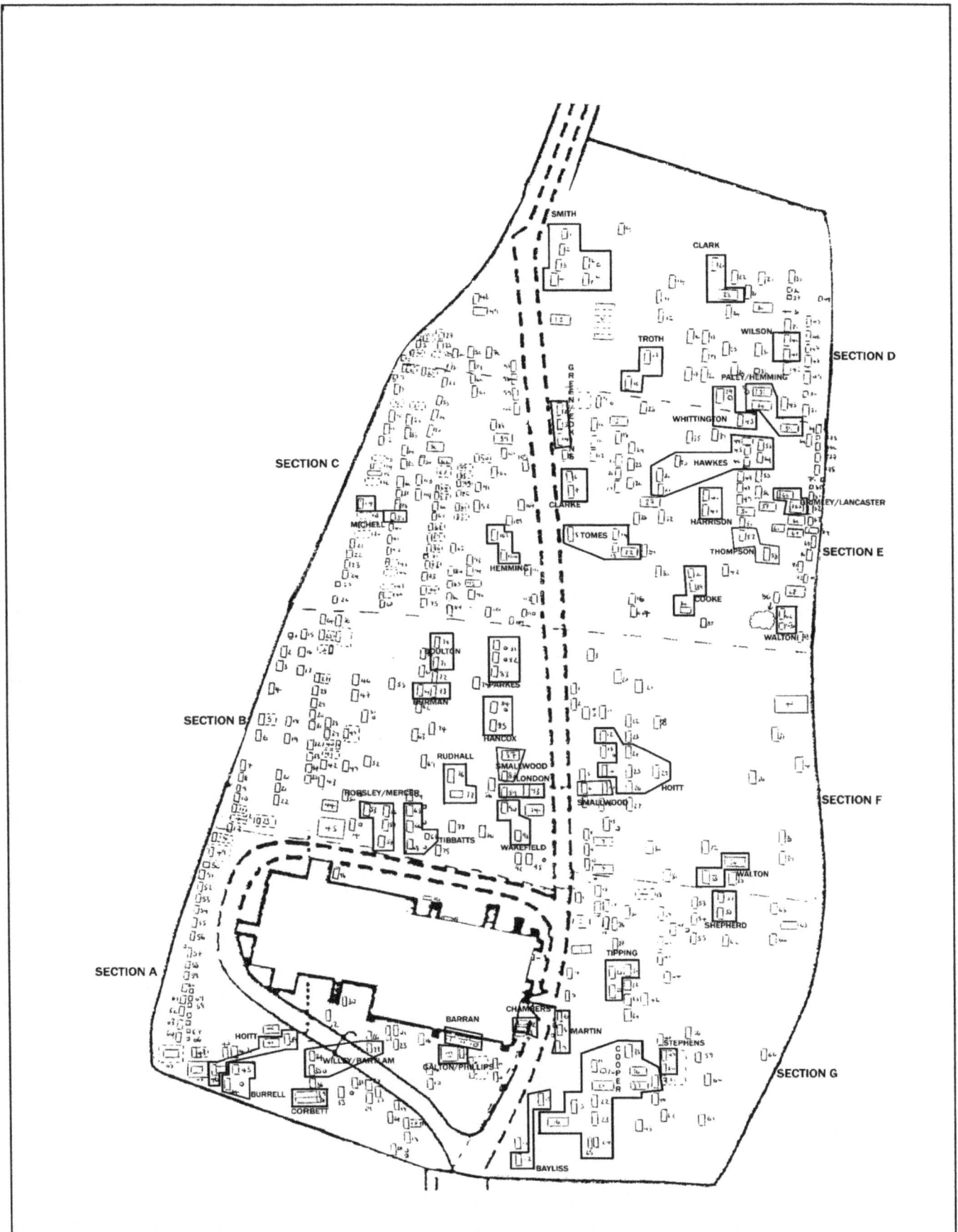

Figure 26. Wootton Wawen: plan of the churchyard showing possible family groups

Chapter Three

ICONOGRAPHY AND ATTITUDES TO DEATH

The different types of memorial found in the churchyards were examined, as was the extent to which the shapes of the stones changed over time. At St Nicholas's church, King's Norton, the most frequently occurring memorial is the upright headstone. This is true in many churchyards because they were the cheapest monument to erect.[1] The earliest memorial recorded is dated 1699 and is short and thick with rounded shoulders (MH641). The next earliest datable headstones are found from 1756 onwards. The earlier headstones are generally much shorter and thicker than later stones (eg MH640) and are found here with slightly rounded or

Figure 27. Kings Norton: examples of Gothic decoration (M739, M740, both of 1870)

bedstead shoulders (so called because their curved top is similar to forms used in contemporary chair backs and bedsteads).[2] Some of these early stones appear to have been inscribed on both sides. From 1760 the triangular pediment (eg ME497) was introduced which was most popular between 1840 and 1850. From the early nineteenth century the headstones slowly start to become taller and thinner and are generally only inscribed on one side. The head of the stone starts to be carved into decorative shapes.

Architectural fashions can be seen to have influenced the monuments in the churchyard at King's Norton. The memorials show the influence of the classical revival with headstones showing a neo-classical simplicity of design. Fashionable during this period were rounded pediments, with a simple arch (eg MH652) or semi-circle (eg MH673), which were popular long-lived shapes. Also popular was the headstone with a central semi-circle at the head and with concave shoulders (MH635), and a headstone with either a sinuous top (eg MH679) or a rounded top with semi-circular shoulders (eg MF738). There was no universal shape found at King's Norton and there appears to have been much experimentation in the nineteenth century.

During the second half of the nineteenth century there were many different shapes of headstones with more experimentation with the top, shoulders and sides. Although the rounded headstone was still used widely at King's Norton, the Gothic revival in architecture in the nineteenth century, which looked back to the medieval period,[3] appears to have inspired many new shapes. Several of the stones become more pointed and very slowly from the 1840s the cross begins to be incorporated into the shape of the top of the headstone (eg MH657). Many of the pointed headstones are accompanied by elaborate Gothic decoration around the top and sides of the stone (MF739 and MF740, Figure 27) and from the

1850s the trefoil starts to be used at the top of the headstone (eg MF759).

The Gothic revival also combines with the religious zeal[4] of the nineteenth century to produce three-dimensional crosses and imitations of the Celtic cross. Crosses begin to be incorporated into the head of the stone from 1850 (eg MF796) and free standing three-dimensional crosses start to be used from about 1860 onwards, and are most commonly found with kerbs. From 1900 imitations of the Celtic cross start to be found at King's Norton. There are 17 altogether and they are most common between 1910 and 1930.

The twentieth century brought a return to smaller headstones, which were mostly rectangular and flat-topped stones. These can initially be seen in the war memorials found at King's Norton (eg MJ905). It was also popular for the headstone to be made into a shape. Popular ones at King's Norton are scrolls and books, and there are also a few rock shapes. Small headstones contrast with the three-dimensional crosses that are still popular during this period.

Kerbs are first found with headstones from 1852, and this combination is the most popular choice of memorial from the early twentieth century. From the late nineteenth century they become a popular form of monument in their own right and there are over 100 from 1910 onwards.

There are six tablets on the church exterior. There are also ten flat stones although it can sometimes be difficult to tell whether a stone is flat, or if a headstone has fallen and now lies where it fell. Fourteen footstones are found with headstones, and 37 footstones on their own, the majority of which are displaced and are now being used as a boundary wall in the churchyard. Four ledger stones are illegible and two ledger stones placed on large bases are found in the early nineteenth century. Ledger stones are recumbent slabs, which are usually rectangular in shape. Originally thought to prevent the soul returning to haunt the living, they were increasingly used to deter body-snatchers.[5]

Larger monuments could be useful to show status and wealth for those families who were not buried inside the church. There are seven chest tombs at King's Norton, dating from 1780 to 1887. The proportions of a chest tomb emphasise the length of the monument. Chest tombs have been popular since the Reformation as they are associated with a social importance superior to that of headstones.[6] The majority of the chest tombs at King's Norton are plain with little decoration. The only exceptions are ME531 and MF756, which have hipped tops and columns at the four corners of the stone, which is typical of the classical revival (Figure 28). Also plain were the five table tombs at King's Norton, dating from 1814 to 1848.

Figure 28. King's Norton: an example of a chest tomb with a hipped top and columns (MF756, date illegible)

Architectural fashions also show their influence in the choice of larger monuments. There are 18 pedestal tombs at King's Norton, dating from 1811 to 1918. Pedestal tombs show the influence of the classical revival with the emphasis on elegance, simplicity and sophistication and are based on the podia of classical buildings and monuments. The proportions are used to emphasise the height of the monument. They have vertical forms, square in section, tapering upwards[7] and are often found with an urn, obelisk or sarcophagus on top. At King's Norton, three have urns on top, two have large angels, one has a broken column, and one has a large cross. Ten of the pedestal tombs from the late nineteenth century onwards have an obelisk on top. Obelisks are often found during this period because the Gothic revival brought an interest in elaborate pinnacles that soared to heaven.[8]

The Gothic revival in architecture also led to the imitation of medieval coped stones (MI826, Figure 29).[9] There are

six coped stones at King's Norton, one dating from 1815 and the rest from 1853 to 1887. Low monuments also

Figure 29. King's Norton: an example of an imitation of a medieval coped stone (MI826, of 1887)

become popular with the Gothic revival. At King's Norton there is one with a hipped top from 1811, and low monuments with hipped tops also appear on four monuments in the mid to late nineteenth century. Four low monuments with crosses on were found in the twentieth century. There is one vault at King's Norton, which is marked only by a small headstone and a very large kerb, and the Grant memorial (MB30, Figure 30), is so large that it does not fit into any of the above categories.

Figure 30. King's Norton: the Grant memorial (MB30, of 1926)

The different types of memorial were also examined at Wootton Wawen. As at King's Norton the most commonly found memorial at Wootton Wawen was the headstone. The earliest headstone is dated 1685 (MB79), and there are three more dated before 1700. After this date headstones appear quite regularly. The earliest stones are short and thick, often with decorative carving in high relief. From 1700 the top of the headstone is a simple arched or bedstead top, with the focus on the carving of the imagery and the decoration surrounding the imagery (eg MC105). The headstones slowly start to become taller and thinner as they did at King's Norton and the influence of the classical revival is shown in the simple round topped (eg MF10) and semi-circular headstones (eg MG8). The triangular pediment (eg MA11) is found at the same period as at King's Norton but is less popular at Wootton Wawen. The slightly sinuous headstone (eg MB51) is more popular than at King's Norton and remains a common choice until the late nineteenth century. Popular at Baswich[10] during this period was the rectangular flat-topped stone. This was not found at King's Norton, but at Wootton Wawen there were a few rectangular flat-topped stones (eg ME45). The central semi-circle starts to be used slightly later than at King's Norton.

There is a little less variety in the shapes of the stones during the nineteenth century than at King's Norton but there are still lots of different styles and experimentation. The influence of the Gothic revival is shown with more pointed headstones starting to appear from the 1840s. By the 1870s these stones are extremely popular. There are some excellent examples of Gothic decoration on the top and sides (MF13, Figure 31), and there are a few examples of the trefoil being used as the top of the headstone (eg MD28).

From the twentieth century pointed stones still appear alongside rectangular stones, but most memorials are now shorter and simpler with less decoration on them. Some of the fashions from this period develop slightly later than at King's Norton. The popularity of new shapes appears much more slowly in Wootton Wawen, with only a few stones in the shapes of books, rocks, and scrolls found from 1900 onwards. More footstones have been found at Wootton Wawen than at King's Norton and Baswich. Twenty-seven were found with headstones, and 32 footstones on their own, mostly in section EE, which is where some stones and fragments of stones were used to make a dry-stone wall. This area is now very overgrown.

Seven flat stones appear sparsely from 1760 onwards and two headstones with body stones were found between 1710 and 1720. Body stones were often used to protect the grave.[11] Kerb stones were not as popular at Wootton Wawen compared with the uniform rows of them found at King's Norton. Kerbs appear with headstones slowly from 1870 onwards but only three are found before 1920. From 1920 to 1940, there are six. Only five kerbs are found on their own from 1910.

Again the Celtic revival is less popular at Wootton Wawen. There are only three Celtic crosses, dating from 1904 onwards, one of which has interlacing on the arms. Two wheel crosses (MF12, Figure 32) were erected in 1855 and 1860 and a cross is incorporated into the top of the headstone on several memorials from 1860. Other three-dimensional crosses became popular at Wootton Wawen with 36 being found from 1860 onwards and two low crosses are found with kerbs.

Figure 31. Wootton Wawen: an example of Gothic decoration (MF13, of 1844)

Figure 32. Wootton Wawen: an example of a wheel cross (MF12, of 1855)

Low monuments appear much later than at King's Norton, dating from 1881 to 1940. There are nine altogether. Low monuments at Wootton predominantly have plain sides and a hipped top. There is one low monument with a convex top, and the monument of the Guinness family is a low monument on a base. Three coped stones are found from 1860 to 1895, two of which are excellent imitations of a medieval coped stone and the other is a modern interpretation of a coped stone.

Chest tombs do not appear until quite late at Wootton Wawen, once burial inside the church was forbidden, with three dating between 1906 to 1937. The earliest tombs are quite plain, having a flat top, with three of them having a column effect on the sides and the inscription on the top of the stone. The chest tombs are decorative, two with slightly hipped tops and one with a rounded top. There is an excellent example of the influence of the Gothic revival with the decoration on a chest tomb dated 1906 (MF40, Figure 33). There are also what appear to be eight plain table tombs dating from 1811 to 1860. The presence of plain tombs concurs with results found at King's Norton and at Baswich, but shows a marked contrast to the decorative flourishes and intricate carving found in areas such as the Cotswolds.[12] There is one ledger stone, but the inscription is illegible. There is also one tiny coffin shaped monument which was for a baby. This is from 1842, and is an early example of a revived medieval style of tomb which was rare without supporting head and footstones (MF19, Figure 34).[13] It appears that the people of Wootton Wawen did not follow all the fashions as there are no pedestal tombs or obelisks there. There is, however, one vault, which is the Galton family vault. This is marked by a large rectangular low monument on a base which is inscribed only with the word 'Galton.'

Figure 33: *Wootton Wawen: an example of a chest tomb with elaborate Gothic decoration (MF40, of 1906)*

Iconography at King's Norton

Considering the variety of stones at King's Norton the iconography was disappointing. Out of 847 stones that could be used to analyse iconography, 272 stones were totally plain except for the inscription. A further 96 stones have only calligraphic and typographic swirls on them which are predominantly used as decoration around the superscription to emphasise the first word of the inscription. A further 87 stones were illegible. Where symbols and decoration were found, they were predominantly on headstones, and throughout the whole period studied the primary decoration is principally found at the top centre of the stone with the inscription below. At King's Norton the stones from the eighteenth and early nineteenth centuries are more aesthetically pleasing than later memorials.

Figure 34. *Wootton Wawen: an example of a very small coffin shaped memorial (MF19, of 1842)*

Burgess argues that memorials are inspired by architecture and church monumental carving.[14] This appears to be true at King's Norton. As the stonemasons followed the trends in the shape of the memorial they used, they also followed the trends in iconography and decoration. In similar studies elsewhere, excellent stones showing images of mortality have been found from the seventeenth century. The earliest datable stone at King's Norton is from 1699 and no symbols of mortality were found. No death's-heads were found there, so no analysis of the transition from death's-heads to cherubs could be seen as found in a similar study in New England.[15] On the earliest memorials the normal location for the primary design was at the top of the headstone, with a frame effect around the inscription. Iconography on the earliest stones, generally carved in high relief, has weathered well.

The earliest iconography found at King's Norton was cherubs. At Baswich,[16] there were 10 memorials decorated with cherubs, so it was possible to trace the changing shape of the wings over time and see how the cherubs became simpler, often with less decoration on them and with the frame effect gradually disappearing. At King's Norton, cherubs were found on four of the 17 memorials recorded before 1800. The earliest was dated 1699 and the latest 1753, but the other two could not be dated because the inscription was illegible so no changes in the shape of them can be traced. Dethlefsen and Deetz argue that cherubs were fashionable in England in the opening decades of the eighteenth century.[17] King's Norton does not therefore appear to be slow in learning about this trend and using it. Cherubs have more human faces than death's-heads,[18] and at King's Norton, the faces are extremely human, almost like portraiture, and the large feathered wings are used to frame the face (Figure 35). Cherubs symbolize immortality and therefore balance the theme of mortality represented by the death's-head. They symbolise a change from the earlier obsessions with time and resignation in the face of mortality to a more hopeful period with thoughts of resurrection to eternal life and salvation.[19] The new images accompany the religious revival and evangelistic renewal from the mid eighteenth century.[20] Cherubs represent the soul of the departed winging its way to heaven[21] and are usually found with other baroque and rococo imagery such as ornamental swags, ribbons, flowers, fruit, leaves and scrolls and curtains. At King's Norton the cherubs are found carved in relief but there is no intricate decoration accompanying the images, the focus being on the top of the stone. MF767 shows two cherubs in the corners of the stone, which may represent the two children of Richard Lea who are commemorated there. MF760 shows three small cherubs at the top of the stone. The inscription is illegible, so it is impossible to tell whether they too represent members of the family.

which are carved in relief. The shell has been used as a symbol of fertility or life-symbols in prehistoric burials and up to recent times.[22] Grapes may symbolize the fruit of a virtuous life and refer to the parable of the vine (John 15:1).[23] During this period there is also a small and simple tree carved in relief on MG596 from 1779. The tree signified life if verdant, like this example from King's Norton (Figure 37), and death, if lopped.[24]

Figure 36. King's Norton: an example of an incised shell which is accompanied by grapes and leaves (ME497, of 1760)

Figure 35. King's Norton: King's Norton: an example of a cherub with wings framing the face (MG565, date illegible)

Figure 37. King's Norton: an example of a tree carved in relief (MG596, of 1779)

Other symbols also appear on monuments during this period which agree with the theme of hope and the growing emphasis on resurrection and life, not death. At King's Norton there is an excellent carving of a shell (Figure 36), on ME497, dating from 1760. It is incised and is accompanied by bunches of grapes and leaves

The classical revival introduces new images. From 1786 the urn is introduced, which is prevalent in the classical symbolism of the eighteenth and nineteenth centuries.[25] Many of the symbols from the classical revival were from pagan antiquity but became fused with Christian imagery and meaning. Neo-classical symbols were tolerated and perhaps embraced[26] by an officially Christian country at a time when traditional Christian symbols such as the cross were trying to overcome their associations with popery. The urn signifies death if closed or draped, but if it is flaming or has garlands it signifies immortality, resurrection or eternal life.[27] There are 11 urns at King's Norton from 1786 to 1873. Seven of the urns are plain, two are draped, and two are accompanied by leaves. One of these is from the early nineteenth century (MF723, Figure 38) where the drapes are carved in relief to flow over the top of the inscription. The urn is accompanied by a small wreath and laurel branches at the top of the memorial. Wreaths become popular with the classical revival and are often used for decoration. The laurel branches may symbolise victory over death. On the pedestal tomb of the Middlemore family the urn is accompanied by shields (ME535). These are quite illegible now, but as members of the family were lords of the manor of Edgbaston, Studley and Hazlewell Hall, they may have shown the family arms.

Figure 38. King's Norton: an example of a draped urn accompanied by wreath and laurel branches (MF723, of 1805)

The theme of hope and belief in salvation and resurrection continued in the early nineteenth century.

Along with the use of urns other symbols were used to represent these thoughts, such as the crown. It is rare to find a crown as an individual feature but this occurs twice at King's Norton in 1819 and 1827 (MF591, Figure 39). The crown is symbolic of honour and glory and symbolizes the kingdom of heaven. It refers to Paul's metaphor to the Corinthians (1 Cor. 9:24-27), when he compared the athlete's award in the foot race to the immortal crown of the Christian life.[28]

Figure 39. King's Norton: an example of a crown (MG591, of 1819)

The classical revival also brought other symbols, such as torches, which are found with a wreath on MH652 at King's Norton dated 1842 (Figure 40). The emblem of the flaming torch was derived from the classical games, where it was handed on to successive runners in the relay race. In this respect it signified life as opposed to those on the memorial at King's Norton which are reversed and therefore signify death and darkness.[29]

Figure 40. King's Norton: an example of reversed torches (MH652, of 1842)

41

Other symbols are found in the mid-nineteenth century. Five doves with olive branches are found at King's Norton, the earliest datable one being from 1859, the latest from 1909 (Figure 41). As Noah's dove it flies with an olive branch in its beak, signifying hope or promise of salvation. During the same period two stones have bunches of wheat on them. The first stone is from 1852 where a small sheaf of corn is in the centre of the headstone, with the top of the headstone draped, and the second is from 1859 and has a large sheaf of corn being reaped by a sickle at the top of the headstone, which signifies the death of the righteous (MH692, Figure 42). Wheat found alone may refer to the good seed in the parable of the sower.[30]

Figure 41. King's Norton: an example of a dove carrying an olive branch (ME508, of 1866)

The Gothic revival not only influenced architecture but also contributed to changes in attitudes to death and a period of high religious seriousness. As it showed its influence over the shape of the stones, it also influenced the iconography on the memorials. Before the Gothic revival, neo-classical symbols dominated representations of death.[31] With the Oxford movement and high church asceticism from the 1830s earlier images were seen as pagan and superstitious.[32] The Gothic revival took place from the 1840s and King's Norton was not slow in following the new fashions.

Traditional Christian symbols began to be used from the late 1840s. Crosses were at first used hesitantly alongside other symbols such as IHS and trefoils. A trefoil (a triple-lobed leaf used in Gothic building and ornament)

symbolizes the Trinity.[33] Crosses were used with trefoils on 13 stones, and two stones used trefoils alone in the 1870s. Small crosses started to appear from 1849. Crosses soon became popular and are incorporated into the shape of the stone from about 1860 onwards. Coinciding with a change towards ritualism in religion and the Gothic revival in architecture the cross became the central motif on monuments in the second half of the nineteenth century. Altogether there are 52 three-dimensional crosses, 17 Celtic crosses, 68 crosses used on their own, and 32 used with other symbols. There were 10 stones with crosses and flowers used together. Popular in the late nineteenth century was the use of a central cross, sometimes on a rock, surrounded by flowers or leaves. It is easy to see the start of standardization with these stones. The five stones from the twentieth century appear to use the flowers more as decoration around the sides of the headstone. Crucifixion scenes were also found on two stones from 1929 and 1932.

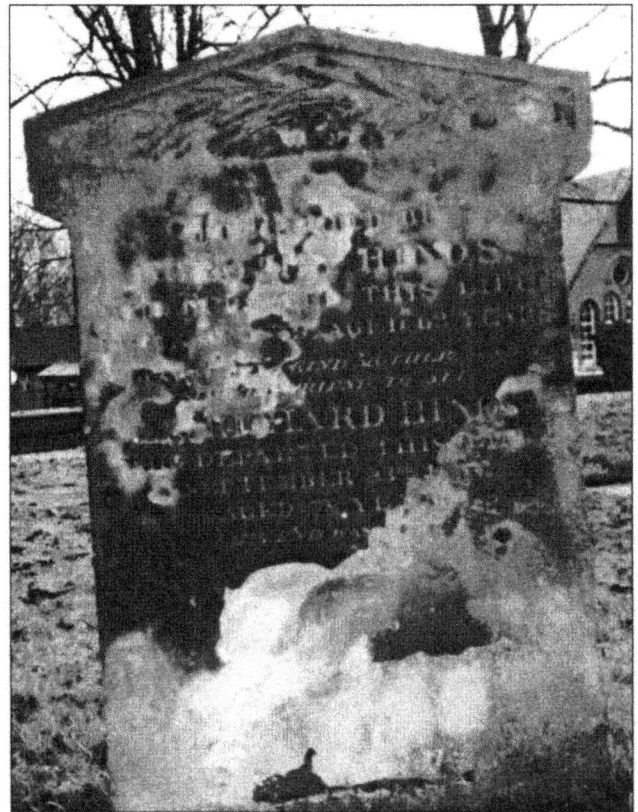

Figure 42. King's Norton: an example of a large sheaf of corn being reaped by a sickle (MH692, of 1859)

Also popular in the iconography at King's Norton was the use of IHS. This is a revival of a late medieval device and was popular with both Anglicans and Catholics in the late nineteenth and early twentieth centuries.[34] IHS, which is used as a Christian symbol and monogram for Jesus, is part transliteration of the Greek form of his name.[35] During a similar study at St Peter's Church in Harborne, we found that IHS was used most frequently before the nineteenth century. Because of the literary form and christocentric character of the symbol it was accepted in the Church of England when the cross was still overcoming its associations with popery.[36] The

42

people of King's Norton were not, however, comfortable using any Christian symbols before 1840, and at King's Norton IHS was not found on a memorial until 1846 when it was used with a cross (MH672). Altogether five stones use crosses and IHS together. Also popular from 1858, and found on 25 stones, was the use of IHS in combination with flowers or ivy leaves. On its own IHS was used from 1860 on a total of 21 stones.

Mixed bouquets of flowers become popular from 1861 at King's Norton, with 43 stones having them as the primary feature at the top of the stone, and 35 more stones using them in combination with IHS or the cross. Single flowers are often found with a cut stem signifying a life cut short. Single flowers are found from 1877 on 18 stones, and are predominantly roses. The rose is an emblem of a paragon of virtue and is associated with the Virgin Mary. Also popular was the passion flower, which is a means of salvation and a symbol of Christ's passion, and the lily which is a symbol of purity.[37] Ivy leaves are used in combination with several other symbols and are found on 13 headstones on their own from the mid to late nineteenth century. Ivy leaves symbolise fidelity because of their clinging nature, and everlasting life because of their evergreen character.[38] Two stones from the late nineteenth century show hands with flowers and one stone from 1914 shows a pair of clasped hands. Hands often point to heaven or signify divine presence and clasped hands signify friendship or brotherly love.[39]

Full-length angels are first seen on headstones in King's Norton from 1871. The earliest is on ME477, on a headstone showing the influence of the Gothic revival with the top of the stone in the shape of a trefoil. This angel is carved in relief and is small and delicate with large feathery wings (Figure 43). The later examples from the twentieth century are not as attractive as this simple one. Three large angels are seen on top of pedestal tombs, and six on headstones. All of the angels have large wings, one of them is praying, and on two of the stones the angels are holding roses. One of the angels is holding a book and two have their hands folded in their lap. Three cherubs appear on ME410 in 1915. Seven stones in the early twentieth century have wreaths on them. Wreaths have been used to signify remembrance but it is likely that these wreaths were for decoration.

Figure 43. King's Norton: an example of a small angel carved in relief (ME477, of 1871)

Similar studies elsewhere have found stones with symbols relating to identities such as heraldry or trade and occupations. No memorials relating to occupation were found at King's Norton. There is one unusual memorial, however, dating from 1926. This is the very large one to the Grant family, who were Roman Catholics (MB30, Figure 30). The family show their faith with a very large cross in the centre of the monument, which is accompanied by the heads of two angels above the two separate inscriptions and what appears to be a knight in the centre of the stone.

Iconography inside the church

At King's Norton the iconography on the memorials inside the church was disappointing. Memorials dated before 1690 are discussed in Appendix 2. Of the others, four were brass plaques. Two memorials were too high up to be seen and 10 were totally plain. The urn is found almost a century earlier than in the churchyard, being on 12 memorials dating from 1698 to 1825, three of which are draped and one is flaming. The earliest memorial with an urn as a symbol is from 1698 and is to the Middlemore family. On another one the urn appears with the Mynors family shield on it, and on two others it appears with cherubs. This shows that the transitions in iconography were not directly from one to another but that symbols were often contemporary. Masons often used new motifs with caution, mingling them with well-tried patterns.[40] On the memorial to John Reeve, gent, the urn is draped and the cherub has a very human face, which is framed by large feathered wings underneath it (MSA13, Figure 44). There are laurel branches at the bottom which, combined with the cherubs, may symbolise victory over death. Another of the earlier memorials is the tablet commemorating the Reverend Hemming and his family, dated 1767. This shows a draped figure holding a book, which is possibly the bible (MN1, Figure 45).

There are family arms on the Burrish family memorial. Arms are also found on the memorial to Sarah East, which is a painted wooden one, and on the two Mynors memorials, and there is a small shield on two of the Lane family memorials. The other Lane family memorial shows roses and passion flowers but is undated.

Gothic decoration appears on some of the memorials from 1852. On the Pountney memorial there is no symbolism, only decoration, and on the Amphlett and Gem memorials, there are small faces on the sides which on the Gem memorial appear to be angels, and on the Amphlett memorial appear to be a man wearing a crown.

Of the latest memorials containing symbolism, the Cartland family memorial is in gold, with angels on it with large gold wings, which hold the inscription, and two birds, one of which is in a shield. The birds may symbolize the holy spirit.[41] The latest iconography found is a small cross in 1893 and a very small IHS in 1904.

Figure 44. King's Norton: a memorial inside the church which shows the use of cherubs and an urn together (MSA13, of 1793)

Figure 45. King's Norton: a memorial inside the church which shows a draped figure holding a book (MNA1, of 1767)

Iconography in Wootton Wawen churchyard

Although the people of Wootton Wawen are quite conservative and reserved in their iconography there are still some aesthetically pleasing pieces. Out of 354 memorials that could be expected to display iconography 82 are completely plain. Another 52 have just decoration on them, predominantly calligraphic and typographic flourishes and scrolls around the superscription to emphasise the first word. Thirty-one stones are totally illegible so it was impossible to tell if they had had any iconography on them. As at King's Norton, the primary decoration was at the top centre of the stone.

Some of the iconography on the earliest stones has weathered well, particularly on the memorials carved in high relief, but for some memorials it is now only possible to find traces of what was originally there. Probably the earliest iconography found at Wootton Wawen is a very worn death's-head (MA15), which cannot be precisely dated because the inscription is illegible (Figure 46). Death's heads have sharper features than cherubs. The death's head is a skeleton with bat-like wings, very unlike the wings of cherubs.[42] They emphasise the closeness of death and suggest mortality through the idea of decomposition. The memorial is illegible and cannot be dated so no transition between death's-heads can be identified at Wootton Wawen. Emblems of mortality are found in many other churchyards, but are rare in this conservative yard. Other emblems of mortality are the remains of a crossed spade and pickaxe tied with a ribbon or crossed with bones (MC105). This signifies the end of earthly power.[43] These appear to either side of the inscription, and there are the remains of either a death's-head or cherub at the top of the stone. The rest of the stone is decorated with flowers and ornament of the Baroque style. Also from the same period is MA22, which shows a hand reaching down, which probably signifies the presence of God.

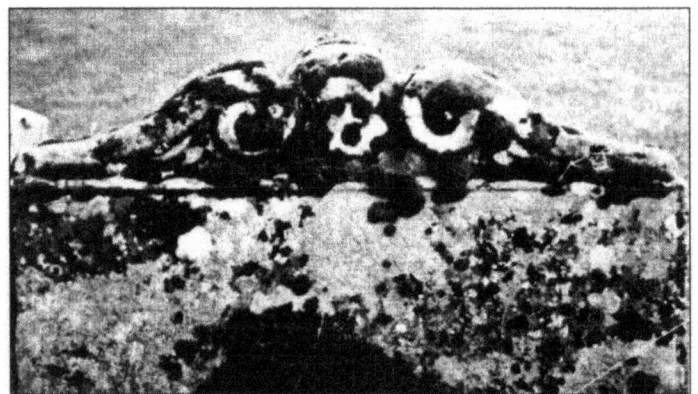

Figure 46. Wootton Wawen: a very weathered example of a death's head (MA15, date illegible)

Representations of death were replaced by gentler images. In contrast to the death's-head, cherubs, which emphasise immortality, are the earliest datable iconography found at Wootton Wawen. Nineteen stones have cherubs on them. The earliest is dated 1685, so they are not behind King's Norton in following fashions, and they last till 1763, just slightly longer than at King's

Norton. They all have either a simple semi-circle or a bedstead top. Each cherub is found in the top centre of the memorial, with a frame effect around the inscription. The earliest has a rounded top, with the cherub at the top of the memorial. The cherub has curly hair and the wings are underneath framing the face. Leaves around the top and sides help to frame the inscription. These early memorials are examples of baroque decoration, having swags, tassels and perhaps fruit (Figure 47). The frame effect does not disappear as it did at Baswich,[44] and decoration continues to be used at Wootton Wawen, but the cherubs become simpler over time and the wings change shape. The latest memorial has two cherubs at the top with fluffy wings underneath framing the face and swags and tassels framing the inscription.

Figure 47. Wootton Wawen: an example of a cherub with baroque decoration of flourishes, swags and tassels (MB68, of 1717)

Another of the earliest stones (MB58, 1686) has ornament of flowers and scrolls and possibly a fleur de lys at the top, which may be symbolic of the Trinity. The next earliest memorials at Wootton Wawen show the influence of the classical revival with the simpler neo-classical design of the late eighteenth and early nineteenth century. These continue the theme of hope and resurrection with symbolic references to heaven such as the trumpets and lyre that appear on a memorial in 1772.[45] Trumpets are also found on two other memorials in the churchyard.

The people of Wootton Wawen were not slow to respond to changes in fashion. There are 11 urns there, with the first appearing in 1781 (five years earlier than at King's Norton) and the last in 1852. Only one of the urns is draped; four of the urns are flaming. Flaming urns signify the resurrection. Five of the urns have scrolls and flourishes around them, and the latest stones have trumpets and crowns in their corners.

At Wootton Wawen traditional Christian symbols are used alongside neo-classical symbols. The cross appears earlier than in similar studies elsewhere and features heavily. This is because Wootton Wawen had a large Roman Catholic community who considered it important to show their denomination. Altogether there are 36 three-dimensional crosses, three Celtic crosses, 27 single crosses, and 16 stones where the cross appears with another symbol. The cross does not enter Anglican iconography after the Reformation until the Oxford movement of the 1830s. At Wootton Wawen a flowered cross (Figure 48) appears on MA23 as early as 1743, signifying the tree of life. As it is accompanied by the epitaph, 'May they rest in peace', it is likely the stone was for a Roman Catholic. After this the cross does not appear with foliage until 1884 when it appears on four memorials with oak leaves and three with flowers, one of them with convolvulus which turns toward the sun, clings and climbs, and symbolizes the good Christian soul.[46] There are none of the mass produced favourites of the cross surrounded by flowers and wheat. Single crosses start to appear, but only rarely, from 1810; they serve almost as ornament and remain popular right through till 1940. Altogether there are 27 stones bearing only crosses, nine of them from the twentieth century. The cross appears with IHS on 10 stones from 1863 onwards. Stones of 1844 and 1855 marked by a plain cross and 'Requiescat in pace' are likely to be among the last Roman Catholic memorials in the yard, the latter commemorating someone who remained faithful to the parish churchyard even after the opening of a separate Roman Catholic cemetery in 1852.

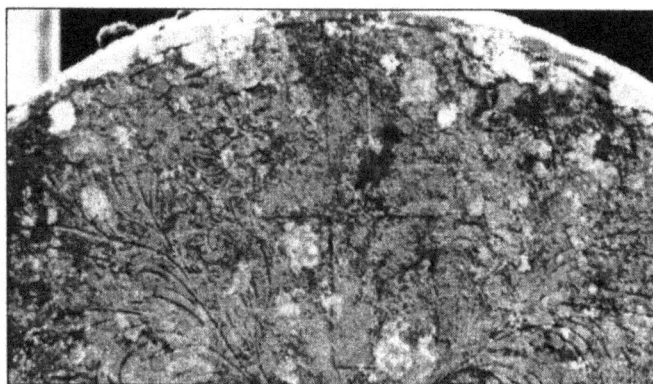

Figure 48. Wootton Wawen: a flowered cross of 1743 (MA23)

Flowers appear on stones as the primary decoration much earlier at Wootton Wawen than at King's Norton and are often enclosed by trefoils or quatrefoils. Single flowers appear on 13 stones and mixed flowers on 10 stones from 1843 onwards. They are predominantly lilies, with a couple of roses, passion flowers, and convolvulus. A rose is also found with a shield on F5. Mixed flowers show the Victorian interest in botanical symbolism with roses, primroses, lilies, oak leaves and ivy. F36 from 1843 mixes roses, flowers, scrolls and trumpets. Flowers are also found in conjunction with other symbols. A large sickle on E37 (Figure 49) reaps passion flowers, poppies, which symbolise eternal sleep, convolvulus, and ears of corn, which symbolize the good Christian gathered in at the harvest. Some of the earlier memorials have excellent examples of flowers, but other more common images are found in the twentieth century, such as the popular hand pointing upwards with ivy leaves and fleur de lys (MB88, Figure 50). The hand is symbolic of the soul's ascent to heaven and ivy leaves are for eternity. Grapes and leaves are found on one memorial in 1865 (E71, Figure 51). Ivy leaves appear on their own on four stones from 1896 onwards suggesting eternity and fidelity.

Figure 49. Wootton Wawen: an example of a large sickle reaping flowers (ME37, of 1882)

The people of Wootton Wawen do not appear to have been comfortable using IHS as a symbol until the mid-nineteenth century, when it is often used in combination with a Gothic shape (Figure 52). IHS is first found on seven stones with ivy and leaves from 1863 onwards, and with the cross on 10 stones. It is also used on its own on 19 stones from 1865 onwards. At this period it is by far the most popular feature but is less popular in the early twentieth century than at King's Norton.

Wreaths are found on two monuments, a headstone on which they appear to be decorative and on the Williams chest tomb (MC56) from 1937 where a ribbon bound wreath is used to frame the monogram W, which is carved in relief on both ends of the tomb.

There are none of the large angels at Wootton Wawen which had begun to be used at King's Norton; instead, flowers, the cross and IHS are used until 1940. There are only two doves with olive branches, one accompanied by a rose and ivy leaves and the other by oak and ivy leaves. The latter appears in 1913, much later than at King's

Norton. There are no memorials showing symbols related to trade or occupation.

Figure 50. Wootton Wawen: an example of a hand pointing to heaven (MB88, of 1899)

Figure 51. Wootton Wawen: an example of the use of grapes and leaves (ME71, of 1865)

46

Figure 52. Wootton Wawen: an example of IHS on a Gothic style memorial (MC111, of 1881)

Symbols of heraldry are rare. Heraldry appears only in the twentieth century when burial within the church is forbidden and families are anxious to display their status. Two of the chest tombs at Wootton Wawen carry interesting decoration. The Fieldhouse memorial (MC89, 1921) has a large cross on its north facing side, on the east there is heraldry (Figure 53), and on the west there is a crown, with a rose and thistle inside it. The crown is a coronet, which should indicate a peerage, but there is no mention of this in the inscriptions. The thistle and the rose could indicate English and Scottish connections. The other chest tomb (MF40, 1906) belonged to the Capewell Hughes family. It carries several different shields showing family arms, which are accompanied by family mottos in Latin.

Iconography inside the church

The iconography inside the church at Wootton Wawen was again disappointing. Out of 49 stones dating from after 1682, five were illegible and 24 were plain. Arms were a valued mark of status and this is shown in the symbolism, as the most frequently occurring iconography inside the church was heraldry. On their own they appear on five memorials, with urns on three memorials from 1698 onwards, and with an urn, laurels and oak tied with ribbons on the monument to Daniel Gaches in the chancel (MCH1, Figure 54). Laurel is symbolic of victory and oak is symbolic of strength. Some people also showed status with their family arms used in combination with fashionable symbols of the time. In 1705 a winged skull and cherubs appear, contemporary with those in the churchyard, together with the family arms on one of the Somervile memorials (MSC4, Figure 55). Heraldry, the

earliest symbol to be found inside the church, is still in use in the late nineteenth century, with arms found with a crown and horn in 1898 (MN5). The coat of arms is that of the Somervile family and the horn and spurs represent William Somervile's celebrity as a huntsman and keeper of his own hounds. Arms are also used in combination with a laurel wreath on the monument to George Henry Capewell Hughes of 1906.

Figure 53. Wootton Wawen: an example of the use of heraldry on the Fieldhouse tomb (MC89, of 1921)

The urn was found on two memorials with other symbols. A large urn appears on a pedestal tomb on one of the Knight memorials in 1765, and one with laurels on another Knight memorial. Laurels also appear on a third Knight memorial, in 1764, in combination with a crown. The urn also appears with other symbols on MSC5 (Figure 56), which commemorates John Phillips and his wife. It is a mixture of classical and Gothic influences, with the pointed architectural surround being used in combination with classical symbols.[47] The urn as a symbol of death is again from classical inspiration, with a lamb placed upon its rim as a Christian symbol of Christ's sacrifice.[48]

The cross is found extremely early inside the church, on two stones with skulls in 1716 and 1718. The skull, which is surrounded by laurels, suggests victory over death. Use of the cross so early in the eighteenth century indicates a Catholic burial. The cross is only found once more, in 1785, and the plain cross stands out clearly and again signifies a Roman Catholic burial. It is interesting that the Smith/Carington family, noted Roman Catholics, do not show this on their monuments.

Figure 54. Wootton Wawen: an urn with laurel branches and heraldry on the monument to Daniel Gaches (MCH1, of 1805)

Figure 56. Wootton Wawen: a mixture of Gothic and Classical influences on the memorial to John Phillips (MSC5, of 1836)

Figure 55. Wootton Wawen: the Somervile family arms, with cherubs and skull (MSC4, of 1705)

Stonemasons

At King's Norton 300 out of 847 stones in the churchyard have the stonemason's name on them; however, 208 are on stones dated between 1900 and 1940 when many of the memorials were plain or merely decorative. More evidence from an earlier period might have allowed certain motifs and styles to be attributed to individual masons or workshops. There are 34 different stonemasons recorded at King's Norton, mainly ones based within the parish. Many of the stonemasons' names are found on only one or two memorials and there are only seven stonemasons who appear on 10 or more stones. The most frequently recorded are H L Marks of Kings Heath, who appears on 42 stones between 1913 and 1940, Locker, of King's Norton and Kings Heath, who appears on 76 stones between 1850 and 1933, and W F Bannock and Sons of Selly Oak and King's Norton, who appear on 67 stones between 1905 and 1940. Locker's work shows much variation. Although there are 24 plain memorials, the other memorials show how the work of a mason changes with the fashions, from an excellent dove in 1859, which appears on a rounded headstone, typical of this period, to a small angel dating from 1871 (Figure 43), which is on a gothic headstone where the top is pointed and in the shape of a trefoil. Both symbols are carved in relief. Also excellent are several of the nine memorials carrying flowers. Later work from

Locker also follows contemporary fashions, with many plain stones, three-dimensional crosses, short headstones with kerbs, and a large angel on top of a pedestal tomb of 1905.

At Wootton Wawen the stonemasons that could be identified were analysed. Among 354 stones there were only 75 that listed the stonemason, and 32 different stonemasons were identified. Most of them were found on only one memorial, and so it was difficult to see if they specialized in certain symbols or decoration; and the majority of stonemasons' names were found on memorials after 1850 and so some of the excellent earlier work was anonymous. However, Keen of Henley, who is recorded on nine stones between 1845 and 1867, shows how a local stonemason and his work follow the influence of fashions in architecture and pattern books. One of Keen's earlier stones shows classical influence with a rounded top and with urn, crown and trumpets in the corners, and his later work shows Gothic influence with the headstone in a more pointed form and with a trefoil at the top. The work of T Davis also shows some variety and the importance of choice in the design, with two of the earliest crosses in 1820 and 1835 and an urn. Two of the plain urns were by Edkins, again of Henley, and some of the excellent later work was done by Checketts of Leamington (1865-1915). The shape of his stones shows the Gothic revival and contemporary images such as a sickle reaping flowers (1882), and a central IHS with trailing ivy on the sides of a pointed stone.

Other denominations

The parish registers at King's Norton clearly show that at least 33 people who were nonconformist and two Roman Catholics are still commemorated on 30 stones in the churchyard. These stones were studied to see if there was anything significant about their iconography to separate them from the others. Of the nonconformist memorials only 16 were decorated, seven with flowers, two with crosses, two with IHS, one with an angel and three with a scroll shape. As the majority of the memorials were from the early twentieth century when flowers were very popular, nothing significant could be found from these results. The large memorial to a Roman Catholic couple dating from 1926 clearly shows their faith with a large cross and angels (Figure 30).

The parish registers at Wootton Wawen show at least seven nonconformists who are still commemorated on surviving memorials. Of these, four had flowers on them, one was in the shape of a Celtic cross, one was in the shape of a scroll on a rock, and one had a cross and ivy on it. With such a small sample of stones, all from between 1870 and 1929, nothing significant was found from these results. No Roman Catholics who were listed in the parish registers were still commemorated on memorials in the churchyard. Many of the stones in the yard with crosses on are, however, likely to be Roman Catholic memorials as the crosses appear much earlier than they would normally do on Anglican stones. This indicates that there may be many more memorials commemorating Roman Catholics than we can identify.

Family Groups

The family groups identified in Chapter 2 were analysed to see if there was any similarity between their stones, which would show the importance of familial affiliation in the choice of memorial. At King's Norton there appear to be only a few family groups that have chosen the same memorials and only one of these groups was from earlier than the twentieth century. This was the Clulee family, who have identical crosses incorporated into the shape of the top of the headstone on three memorials in section G. Of the twentieth century families, both of the Tay memorials are Celtic crosses, and both of the Fryer memorials are Celtic crosses and kerbs with roses.

At Wootton Wawen, it appears to have been more important for people to be together in death as in life. There are 14 family groups who appear to have chosen the same memorials. For three of these family groups it is stones dating from the same period that are the same. An example of this is the Cooper family who have urns on four of their earliest memorials. For the other 11 family groups all of their memorials show identical designs. Similarities range from the conservatism of four of the families who all have identical plain stones, to the Tibbatts family, who have three memorials in the early eighteenth century, which all have cherubs on them, two of which are totally identical stones, in baroque style with tassels and garlands of fruit and flowers (Figure 47). Other families choosing similar memorials are the Smallwoods who have identical low monuments, the Clarkes with their floral ornament, the Waltons with IHS, the Lancasters who have IHS and foliage and the Whittingtons who merely have plain crosses at the top of their stones. These results emphasise the importance of family solidarity to the people at Wootton Wawen, which was identified in the discussion of the development of the churchyard in Chapter 2.

Birmingham City Centre

The iconography of 1279 memorials from two municipal cemeteries and four churchyards in Birmingham city centre was recorded so as to discover if there was a wider variety of iconography in an urban context and if townspeople were quicker to learn about and utilise the trends in fashion than at King's Norton and Wootton Wawen. We have already seen that the people from both of these areas do not seem to have been particularly slow in learning about new trends and following them. Unfortunately no comparisons with gravestones from inner cities could be done before 1840 because many of Birmingham's oldest churches have been demolished, or the churchyards have been turned into gardens.

The earliest memorials found in the new cemeteries had classical symbols and styles, possibly because many people still associated Gothic decoration with papism. At

King's Norton, from 1850 the cross predominates as the most popular symbol in every decade, followed by flowers and IHS. At Wootton Wawen the cross again predominates, although flowers and IHS are also extremely popular in several of the decades. Most popular by far at Warstone Lane and Key Hill in Birmingham is the use of flowers. At Key Hill there are a few examples of single flowers, such as lilies or roses broken at the stem, but flowers are mainly shown in mixed bouquets. Flowers in a bowl were introduced at both Key Hill and Warstone Lane from about 1860, along with a draped headstone with flowers on it. Also popular were a hand pointing up to heaven, surrounded by flowers and wheat, and a central cross on a rock surrounded by flowers (Figure 57). Many stones also use ivy leaves as the central ornament.

Figure 57. Birmingham, Warstone Lane: an example of a cross on a rock surrounded by flowers (1880)

A weeping willow appears as late as 1878 (Figure 58). Weeping willows were popular during the classical revival, symbolising the theme of grief and mourning. At both Key Hill cemetery and Warstone Lane, the urn is found on top of many of the pedestal tombs throughout the nineteenth century. Although new symbols were introduced, "heathen" emblems had taken hold and the urn survived the condemnation of the nineteenth century in many churchyards and cemeteries.[49] There are also a few examples of scythes reaping flowers at Key Hill. One memorial with acorns on it may symbolise strength.

The number of memorials carrying IHS and the cross is relatively very small. Between 1880 and 1890, for example, at least 131 stones at Key Hill use flowers in some form as the key symbol, whereas IHS is found on only eight stones and the cross on only six. Aside from this there is very little symbolism. There are a few examples of shields, doves, wreaths and a couple of anchors, which are a symbol of hope, and there are a couple of large monuments with women clinging to the cross, inspired by a Calvinist hymn of 1775 which stated 'Nothing in my hand I bring, simply to thy cross I cling.'

At Warstone Lane cemetery, the results are similar. Christian symbols are used slightly more than at Key Hill cemetery; in the 1870s, flowers are found in some form on 46 stones and IHS is used on 37 stones. After 1880, however, flowers are found more predominantly than anything else. On a few stones single flowers such as roses are found, but they are mostly in mixed bunches. Again the hand pointing up to heaven and the cross on the rock surrounded by flowers are popular pieces. Also popular was wheat on its own, and there are also a few scythes reaping the flowers. IHS is still popular during this period but accounts for only a third of the stones that flowers are found on. As at Key Hill the cross is found only on a small number of stones. There are a couple of large angels and a man with a cross and a book, which may be the bible.

Figure 58. Birmingham, Key Hill: an example of the influence of the classical revival with the use of a weeping willow (1878)

The unfortunate thing about many of the memorials at both Key Hill and Warstone Lane is that by the late nineteenth century the memorials clearly show the impact of mass production. At Warstone Lane, however, there are a few unique pieces in amongst the rows of similar stones. On memorial stones from 1860 onwards there can be found examples of a small bird, grapes, torches, five doves and two faces, which are possibly biblical. There is also some room for individuality with an excellent harp and violin and a biblical scene. The violin (Figure 59) was erected by the deceased's colleagues from the musical profession in Birmingham. The violin is surrounded by leaves, which perhaps symbolise an everlasting life. Unique stones are not, however, always aesthetically pleasing: a large tree trunk, made by the family of the deceased, stands out starkly amongst the rows of identical headstones.

At Ward End there are only 20 memorials remaining. The results again show flowers to be predominant, appearing on 12 of the memorials, but as there are so few left little could be drawn from this. The same is true of the few remaining memorials recorded from St Paul's and St Philip's churchyards. At St Joseph's Roman Catholic church,[50] Nechells, 123 memorials were used to look at iconography and the findings were very different, with IHS being the most predominant symbol, and from 1880 flowers and the cross were used in the same proportions. Although crucifixion scenes are rare, there are two at Nechells from the 1870s (Figure 60), earlier than those at King's Norton, and an angel is found as early as 1850.

Figure 59. Birmingham, Warstone Lane: a violin on a memorial erected by the deceased's colleagues from the music profession (1900)

Figure 60. Birmingham, Nechells: an example of a crucifixion scene (1876)

There was also an excellent example of the Virgin Mary (Figure 61). Flowers are used later at Nechells, being initially found in 1870 with the cross. The memorials from this Roman Catholic churchyard hint at what might have been learnt if earlier memorials were available.

The analysis of memorials in the city centre has shown that even with mass production and standardisation choice is still important. There are still individual designs in amongst the masses of uniform stones and religion can still heavily influence the design of the monument. The heavy use of flowers could be explained in several ways. As the people in Key Hill were predominantly non-conformist[51] and also used a lot of classical imagery it is likely that they were happier with flowers on their memorials than anything too religious. This was

combined with the fashion for flowers and mass production of the period, which starts to show itself slightly later at King's Norton and Wootton Wawen. The influence of religious feeling on the memorials agrees with the results found in the Roman Catholic churchyard at Nechells where biblical and Christian symbols were in heavy use.

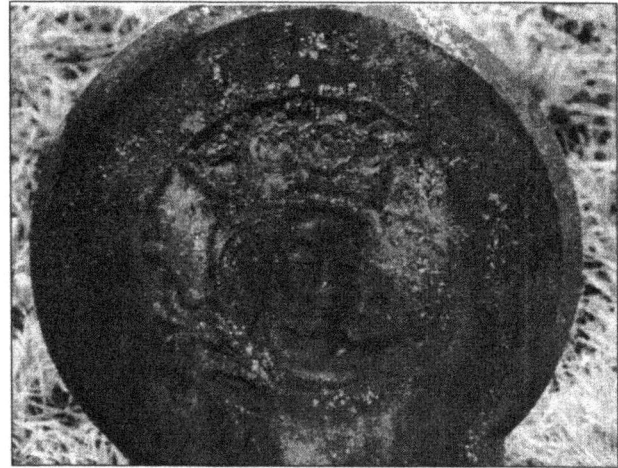

Figure 61. Birmingham, Nechells: an example of the Virgin Mary (1876)

The results from King's Norton and Wootton Wawen show us that many people in both areas remained conservative with plain or purely decorative memorials being popular throughout. There were still, however, some people who used the stones as a means of expressing explicit religious and social feelings. Architectural fashions and designs from pattern books influenced the work of the masons,[52] who developed their own styles and designs and introduced these into the area. By the mid-nineteenth century there were a large number of pattern books in circulation from which monumental masons derived inspiration.[53] This was combined with the changing religious atmosphere, which informed the design and conditioned the development of monumental forms.[54] Until the end of the nineteenth century much of the iconography shows thoughts about religion. This is not surprising considering that religion exercised a pervasive influence on the life of England during this period.[55]

Burgess argues that in remote country districts, changes in style and imagery manifest themselves later than in urban areas, which are more sensitive to the whims of fashion.[56] This may be true in some areas of the country but King's Norton and Wootton Wawen do not appear to be particularly slow in following the fashions, as the same designs are generally found in their graveyards contemporary with those from the city of Birmingham. The finest work is found until about the mid-nineteenth century. After this point large firms start to standardize their designs, and ordering increasingly takes place from illustrative catalogues.[57] Individual craftsmanship becomes a rarity and the standardisation of memorials can be seen easily at King's Norton where stones from this time begin to have a uniformity (Figure 62). Mass production and commercialism become combined with secularisation and the de-christianization of the people,[58] and it is likely that symbols have lost much of their meaning by the end of the nineteenth century.

Figure 62. King's Norton: an example of the standardization of the twentieth century

The iconography on the memorials has been extremely useful in looking at attitudes to death and changes in religious feeling. Chapter 4 will continue with this investigation, using the epitaphs to see what they can tell us and how they change over time.

[1] B Bailey, *Churchyards of England and Wales* (1987), p. 123, cited hereafter as Bailey, *Churchyards*
[2] H. Mytum, *Recording and Analysing Graveyards* (2000), p. 7
[3] J. Rugg, 'From reason to regulation: 1760-1850', in eds. P. Jupp and C. Gittings, *Death in England: An Illustrated History* (1999), pp. 202-230 (p. 226), cited hereafter as Rugg, 'Reason to regulation'
[4] K. Lindley, *Of Graves and Epitaphs* (1965), p. 100, cited hereafter as Lindley, *Graves*
[5] *Ibid.* p. 40
[6] F. Burgess, *English Churchyard Memorials* (1963), p. 130, cited hereafter as Burgess, *Memorials*
[7] Lindley, *Graves*, p. 41
[8] C. Brooks, *Mortal Remains: The History and Present State of the Victorian and Edwardian Cemetery* (1989), p. 61, cited hereafter as C. Brooks, *Mortal Remains*
[9] Burgess, *Memorials*, p.125
[10] I. Shorters, 'A study of the grave memorials of Holy Trinity Church, Baswich, Staffordshire' (University of Birmingham, unpublished BA dissertation, 2000), p. 47, cited hereafter as Shorters, 'Baswich'
[11] S. Bassett, *The Wootton Wawen Project: Report Number 5* (1987), pp. 8-13 (p. 9), cited hereafter as Bassett, *Wootton Wawen 5*
[12] *Ibid.* p. 9
[13] Burgess, *Memorials*, p. 130
[14] *Ibid.* p. 30
[15] E. Dethlefsen and J. Deetz, 'Death's heads, cherubs and willow trees: experimental archaeology in colonial cemeteries', *American Antiquity*, 31 (1966), pp. 502-510, cited hereafter as Dethlefsen and Deetz, 'Cherubs'
[16] Shorters, 'Baswich', pp. 52-53
[17] Dethlefsen and Deetz, 'Cherubs', p. 507
[18] *Ibid.* p. 503
[19] *Ibid.* p. 506
[20] J. Dove, 'A Comparison of gravestones in two country churchyards', in *Proceedings of the Geologist's Association*, Volume 103:2 (1992), pp. 143-154 (p.145)
[21] A. Wager, 'Three centuries of death: a Study of the attitudes reflected in Gravestones in Shenstone (Staffs) Churchyard', *Transactions of the South Staffordshire Archaeological and Historical Society*, 19 (1979), pp. 47-55 (p. 48), cited hereafter as Wager, 'Three centuries of death'
[22] Burgess, *Memorials*, pp. 183-184
[23] Bassett, *Wootton Wawen 5*, p. 11
[24] Burgess, *Memorials*, pp. 184-185
[25] Wager, 'Three Centuries of death', p. 48
[26] Bailey, *Churchyards*, p. 27
[27] B. Kemp, *Church Monuments* (1985), p. 26
[28] Burgess, *Memorials*, p. 178
[29] *Ibid*, p. 184
[30] *Ibid*, p. 179
[31] Rugg, 'Reason to Regulation', p. 206
[32] J. Morley, *Death, Heaven and the Victorians* (1971), pp. 53-62
[33] Bassett, *Wootton Wawen 5*, p. 11
[34] *Ibid.* p. 11
[35] *Longman Concise English Dictionary* (1985), p. 696
[36] G. Rowell, 'Nineteenth-century attitudes and practices', in ed. G. Cope, *Dying, Death and Disposal* (1970), pp. 49-57 (p. 52)
[37] Lindley, *Graves*, p. 108
[38] Bassett, *Wootton Wawen 5*, p. 11
[39] Burgess, *Memorials*, p. 180
[40] *Ibid*, p. 122
[41] Lindley, *Graves*, p. 107
[42] Esdaile, *English Monumental Sculpture*, p. 29
[43] B. Kemp, *English Church Monuments* (1980), p.176
[44] Shorters, 'Baswich', p. 54
[45] S. Bassett, *The Wootton Wawen Project: Report Number 3* (1985), pp. 15-16 (p. 15)
[46] Bassett, *Wootton Wawen 5*, p. 11
[47] S. Bassett, *The Wootton Wawen Project: Report Number 6* (1988), p. 14
[48] Burgess, *Memorials*, p. 180
[49] Lindley, *Graves*, p. 100
[50] ed. W. B. Stephens, The Victoria History of the Counties of England, *Warwick, Volume VII: The City of Birmingham* (1964), p. 408
[51] C. Upton, *A History of Birmingham* (1993), pp. 139-141
[52] H. Lees, *English Churchyard Memorials* (2000), p. 51
[53] Burgess, *Memorials*, pp. 167-168
[54] L. Weaver, *Memorials and Monuments* (1915), p. 394
[55] F. Bédarida, *A Social History of England 1851-1990* (1991), p. 85, cited hereafter as Bédarida, *Social History*
[56] Burgess, *Memorials*, p. 114
[57] *Ibid.* p. 115
[58] Bédarida, *Social History*, p. 90

Chapter Four

EPITAPHS

In the churchyards

The epitaphs on the memorial stones were studied at both King's Norton and Wootton Wawen. The analysis will not be comparative, but will draw on all of the memorials recorded in both churchyards to look at what epitaphs can tell us and how the theme and tone of them change over time. Epitaphs can be of great interest, because just as the iconography found in both churchyards shows changes in attitudes to death and religious feeling over time, so epitaphs too are a possibly unique source providing insights into attitudes to death during this period. Many of the inscriptions in both churchyards are only brief and factual, containing no epitaph. At King's Norton 202 of the memorials contain inscriptions which give only factual information about the deceased such as name, age and date of death and at Wootton Wawen 107 of the stones contain only this information.

The earliest epitaphs, found from the late seventeenth century, voice people's concerns about mortality and their obsession with the shortness of life and the closeness of death. There is little mention of an afterlife or resurrection in the epitaphs of this period. At the same time the themes of mortality and death are also being shown in the memorials' iconography. The earliest iconography found at Wootton Wawen contained symbols of mortality such as the deaths-head, a spade and a pickaxe. The earliest epitaphs complement the iconography of this period, therefore, often being messages from the deceased warning passers by to live a good life because life is short and death will come to all of us. This epitaph is of 1682:

> 'All yow that come
> My grave to see
> Even as I am
> Soe shall yow bee
> May we therefore
> Live godly still
> Then welcom death
> Com when it will.'(MA29)

The theme and tone of this message was the most common on the earliest stones, and continue to be found on memorials in the eighteenth century. Epitaphs of this period show resignation in the face of mortality, reminding the reader of the shortness of life and the need to prepare for death, such as one from 1714:

> 'Death you see that none will spare
> Therefore let young and old prepare
> For it will come assuredly
> And some shall dy as young as I.'
> (Wootton Wawen, MB66)

Other messages of this period show the belief in the power of death to separate people and the concern about whether they would see each other again. This epitaph from 1781 shows the unhappiness of a husband being parted from his wife:

> 'Short and uncertain is our bliss below
> None could be happier in this vale of woe
> True mutual love had soften'd every care
> When mournful death divorc'd the happy pair.'
> (Wootton Wawen, ME47)

Warnings continue on memorials found at the very beginning of the nineteenth century. Epitaphs warn of the shortness of life and emphasise the lack of man's power, from the short 'Prepare to meet thy God' (Amos 4:12), to others such as:

> 'A sudden change hath we befell
> I had not time to bid my friends farewell
> Reader! Prepare, make no delay
> You know not the hour nor the day.'
> (King's Norton, ME530, of 1846)

Epitaphs from this period also continue to stress human frailty and the need to be virtuous and live a good life for salvation:

> 'Alas how frail is mortal man
> His date on earth is but a span
> Then look and learn as you pass by
> Both how to live and how to die.'
> (King's Norton, MH604, of 1809)

Warnings about the shortness of life continue on a few memorials during the late nineteenth century, such as

> 'Be ye ready also for the
> Son of man cometh at an hour
> When ye think not,'[1]
> (Wootton Wawen, MF16, of 1854)

and some people still felt it was important to show that because life was short it was necessary to prepare for death:

> 'Set thine house in order for thou
> Shalt die and not live.'[2]
> (King's Norton, MF793, of 1865)

Popular short expressions of this theme in the late nineteenth century were 'In the midst of life we are in death'[3] and 'Prepare to meet thy God,'[4] but by this time warnings are no longer the most commonly found theme on epitaphs.

The obsession with mortality was slower to disappear from the epitaphs than in the iconography. Warnings are found in use alongside iconography with new themes but are less frequent in the nineteenth century. The majority of epitaphs however show values regarding death that change in harmony with the designs. As the symbols of iconography change with fashions in architecture and changes in religious attitudes, the theme and tone of the epitaphs changes also. From the late eighteenth century the iconography of the memorials becomes more sentimental, lighter and more hopeful. Representations of death are replaced with gentler images such as cherubs, and there is a growing emphasis on resurrection and life, not death. The same thoughts about immortality and salvation also begin to be expressed in the epitaphs with a few hopeful messages being found on memorials in the eighteenth century which start to talk about life beyond death. From then onwards epitaphs also become more personal and sentimental. Two of the earliest references to heaven and the afterlife are found at Wootton Wawen in the early eighteenth century, one of which is

'Death is swallowed up in victory.'[5]
(MB97, of 1717)

The other is combined with the virtues of the deceased on A15:

'Reader Rebekah is inclosd here
Beloved of her husband and children dear
Provident patient and virtuous
Unto her righteous kind and courteous
Well may she rest and undis
Tirbed sleep on
Till the great morn of the
Resurrection.'

During this period few people were as confident about the afterlife as these epitaphs indicate because although many epitaphs show hopeful and more positive attitudes to death in the nineteenth century, the earliest ones show uncertainty. During the late eighteenth and early nineteenth centuries epitaphs begin to contain references to the afterlife and resurrection and the idea that the deceased is with God, but these are initially quite tentative and hesitant. These epitaphs are found at a time when the iconography on the memorials is also becoming more positive and showing hope and belief in heaven, resurrection, and victory over death with the use of images such as trumpets, urns and the crown. The theme that death brings rest or peace is found with the epitaph RIP on a stone marked with a cross as early as 1766 on what is probably a Roman Catholic memorial. After this time other epitaphs with this tone are not found until the early nineteenth century when they are tentative such as,

'In hopes of a place of rest.'
(MD13, of 1810)

Also from the late eighteenth and early nineteenth centuries a few people began to be more positive about death, with messages showing that although they were sad at the loss of a loved one, they hoped to be reunited with them:

'Dear girl farewell nor let a mother's grief
Or sister's tears despair of Heaven's relief
But wait that solemn day that shall restore,
And prove their child not lost but gone before.'
(King's Norton, ME509, of 1818)

The people of both King's Norton and Wootton Wawen stressed the importance of faith for salvation in epitaphs from the early nineteenth century:

'Ye grieve for me alas it is in vain
For your great loss is my eternal gain
I hope my peace was made with God before
I went from hence and shall be seen no more.'
(Wootton Wawen, MA26, of 1804)

Other epitaphs emphasised the importance of belief for salvation:

'Jesus said I am the resurrection and the life
He that believeth in me, though he were dead
Yet shall he live'.[6]
(King's Norton, MH611, of 1847)

Epitaphs conveying this theme remained popular, particularly after the mid-nineteenth century. Also becoming more frequent during this period were references to judgement day, heaven and the afterlife. The earliest ones are hesitant and hopeful such as,

'Make hast to Christ make no delay
No one knows his dying day
Go hence my friends and shed no tears
We must lie here till Christ appears
And when he comes we hope to have
A joyful rising from the grave.'
(King's Norton, MG596, of 1789)

The iconographical symbols in the mid-nineteenth century continue with the positive theme. The urn is still in frequent use and alongside this symbols are used such as torches signifying life and doves signifying hope or promise. From the mid-nineteenth century people start to use traditional Christian symbols such as the cross. The theme and tone of the epitaphs again changes to complement the iconography, reflecting changes in attitudes towards death. Epitaphs with hopeful messages about resurrection and salvation are now more frequent, and as the nineteenth century progressed people became less tentative and more certain about the afterlife. This is reflected in the epitaphs which become more explicitly religious, with stronger expressions of faith. They show faith in God and the afterlife, and more confidence in resurrection and the grounds of Christian salvation, and they are more positive and definite in their beliefs. The change can possibly be seen as a product of a period of growing religious seriousness attributable to the Methodist movement, the educational value of the Sunday-school movement and the evangelical and Anglo-Catholic revivals of the first half of the nineteenth century.[7] Epitaphs about resurrection and salvation sometimes appear with strong messages of faith such as:

'I know that my redeemer lives
And on the earth shall stand,
And tho' to worms my flesh he gives
My dust lies in his hand.'[8]
(King's Norton, ME493, of 1849)

By the late nineteenth century the tone is even more positive, with messages such as:

'As in Adam all die
Even so in Christ shall all be made alive,'[9]
(Wootton Wawen, MA40, of 1887)

and

'And when the chief shepherd shall appear they will
Receive a crown of glory that fadeth not away.'[10]
(King's Norton, ME481, of 1890)

For many people their beliefs were now certain with epitaphs such as:

'He is gone. He is gone to the regions of light.
'He was with us today, he is in heaven tonight.'
(King's Norton, MH714, of 1898)

Also popular by the end of the nineteenth century were references to judgement day. A popular inscription was 'Until the dawn breaks and the shadows flee away.'[11] Many of the epitaphs referring to judgement day suggest that the dead were sleeping until the chosen time:

'Her flesh shall slumber in the ground
Till the last trumpets joyful sound
Then burst the chains with sweet surprise,
And in her saviours image rise.'
(King's Norton, MD857, of 1857)

As the general tone of the epitaphs becomes more hopeful and positive from the mid-nineteenth century, epitaphs containing references to the deceased being with God become popular. These were often used for the deaths of children. Popular epitaphs were 'Safe in the arms of Jesus,'[12] 'With Christ which is far better,'[13] and 'Suffer little children to come unto me.'[14] Many epitaphs also give the impression that there was a sense that death meant that the people had come full circle, with images that the body is dust which returns to the earth and the soul goes to God:

'The dust shall return to the earth as it
Was; and the spirit shall return
Unto God who gave it.'[15]
(Wootton Wawen, ME14, of 1837)

As people became less cautious in their epitaphs about the afterlife from the mid-nineteenth century, many inscriptions are found emphasising the idea that death brings a better life, an end to suffering and a move from darkness into light. Favourite epitaphs by the end of the nineteenth century were 'Blessed are the dead which die in the Lord,'[16] and 'Come unto me, all ye that labour and are heavy laden, and I will give you rest,'[17] but there are also some more individual expressions of this such as:

'I reckon that the sufferings of this present time are not worthy to

Be compared with the glory which shall be revealed in us.'[18]
(Wootton Wawen, MB87, of 1883)

An interesting epitaph for children was found at Wootton Wawen on MD21, of 1840:

'The lamb which is in the midst
Of the throne shall feed them and
Shall lead them unto living fountains
Of waters and God shall wipe
Away all tears from their eyes.'[19]

As the belief in resurrection and the afterlife becomes more certain the idea of meeting loved ones in heaven is now more definite:

'On the resurrection morning soul and body meet again
No more sorrow, no more weeping, no more pain,
On that happy Easter morning all the graves the dead restore
Father sister child and mother meet once more.'[20]
(King's Norton, MI808, of 1898)

For many people it was important to show the importance of God in death, that death was a result of God's will and that God called people from the earth to him so that death should not be seen in a negative light:

'He is absent from those who have loved him
It was Jesus who called him away
He has gone to the Lord who redeemed him
From night to the splendours of day.'
(Wootton Wawen, MA33, of 1889)

Many of the epitaphs containing references to the power of God are found from the mid-nineteenth century. A popular short expression of God's will was, 'Thy will be done'[21] but there are others such as,

'So he bringeth them into the haven
Where they would be'
(Wootton Wawen, MG16, of 1878)

Other epitaphs from this period show the importance of God and emphasise that there was no need to be scared about death because he would be with you. This theme is shown on a few memorials in the late nineteenth and early twentieth centuries as:

'Yea though I walk through the valley
Of the shadow of death
I will fear no evil.'[22]
(King's Norton, MI823, of 1918)

Accompanying the idea of the power of God is the theme that God is a physician and takes away pain. The idea of illness and suffering is often shown in this popular epitaph, or a variation of it, found on several stones from 1763 until the mid-nineteenth century:

'Affliction sore long time I bore
All earthly help was vain,

Till death did seize, and God did please,
To ease me of my pain.
Unto my saviours arms I flew.'

Other epitaphs speak of the dead as enduring illness because of faith, or, on the memorial to an elderly lady, as calling to God and being answered:

'I waited patiently for the Lord
And he inclined unto me and heard my calling.'[23]
(Wootton Wawen, MD40, of 1861)

For children, God was seen as granting their requests to see him:

'Though young in years, yet ripe in grace
They longed to see their saviours face
He kindly granted their request
And took them to his heavenly rest.'
(King's Norton, MD854, of 1829)

By the late nineteenth century epitaphs have a very comforting tone. Epitaphs of this period demonstrate how far the tone has changed from the harsh warnings about mortality and the shortness of life found on the earliest memorials. Most popular are the images that death was a restful experience. Commonly found are 'Rest in Peace' and 'His end was peace,'[24] and there are others like:

'There remaineth therefore a rest to the people of God'.[25]
(King's Norton, MF745, of 1876)

As time goes by epitaphs also become more personal. From the mid-nineteenth century ever more people felt that it was important to show their feelings about the deceased in the epitaph with messages of remembrance. Most are concerned with the idea that the dead will not be forgotten. Other personal epitaphs show the sorrow of those left behind, with messages of grief. These were extremely popular in the late nineteenth and early twentieth centuries, from the short 'In life beloved, in death lamented,' to longer epitaphs such as:

'Oh not lost but gone before us,
Let them never be forgot,
Sweet their memory to the lonely,
In our hearts they perish not.'
(King's Norton, MF778, of 1879)

Other epitaphs found from the mid-nineteenth century are from the point of view of the deceased, with prayers to God to look after those they have left behind:

'O thou whose mercy is so great,
Whose grace is unconfined,
Still guard with thy protecting hand
The babes I've left behind,
Engraven deeply on their hearts,
Let thy commandments be,
That there may reign within their breast
No other God but thee.'
(King's Norton, MF736, of 1852)

Although most people followed the general trends in epitaphs from messages of mortality, to tentative and hesitant messages of hope, to more definite and certain messages about the afterlife, there were people throughout the entire period of study who did not show their attitudes to religion and death in the epitaph, but instead felt that it was important to show the virtues of the deceased. Popular choices for these people were epitaphs which had been especially composed for memorials. Personal epitaphs are found from the seventeenth century, extolling virtues of the dead:

'My mother deare
Lyth buried here
Rests from al hir paine
Shee was belov'd
Of Neighbours deare
Yet death to hir was gaine.'
(Wootton Wawen, MA28)

These are often found with messages of remembrance such as this memorial at King's Norton which tells us about Mr Thomas Raybold:

'The mildness of his manners
And the benevolence of his disposition
Procured to him when living
The friendship and esteem
Of all who knew him and will render
His death long and deeply regretted.'
(ME529, of 1818)

Sometimes it was even important to the people to demonstrate the virtues of children such as on this epitaph from 1832,

'Here rests in peace, a much lamented child,
Of manners gentle and of temper mild
Prompt to obey, in wisdom's path he trod
And early knew his saviour and his God.'
(King's Norton, ME542)

The Gothic revival rebelled against this praise of the dead. Reverend F. E. Paget in his *Tract Upon Tombstones* of 1843, argued that the proper type of epitaph 'should be characterised by Christian humility, kindness, and a disposition to say too little rather than too much,'[26] but many people continued to praise the virtues of the deceased. A popular choice for extolling virtues in the nineteenth century was:

'Her ways were ways of
Pleasantness, and all her
Paths were peace.'
(Wootton Wawen, ME39, of 1873)[27]

But also popular were individual praises such as,

'She was a crown to her
Husband, and her price
Was far above rubies,'[28]

which accompanies the epitaph above. Some people, however, preferred to use the space to rail against praising people on monuments,

'Praises on tombstones are words idly spent
A mans good name is his best monument.'
(Wootton Wawen, MB86, of 1857)

There are a few memorials in each churchyard where the epitaph uses a metaphor to hide the reality of death. These were popular for the deaths of children, depicting them as flowers. The earliest dates from 1686, on a memorial to a child:

'The rigid north soon sweeps the rose
Away
Which was but now so young and
So gay
Just so too early fate deaths
Mighty hand
This blooming flower nipt and
Laid it in the sand
Whence reader know youth
Strength nor beauty can
Extend beyond the limits of a span.'
(Wootton Wawen, B58, of 1686)

Also popular was to depict the child as a lamb, shown in the epitaph,

'He shall gather the lambs with his
Arms and carry them in his bosom,'[29]
(King's Norton, MD819, of 1874)

Metaphors are also found on adult memorials:

'She had faded gently from the sight as flowers
To summer fade. She vanished as the rainbow
After sultry showers. She sunk pale and lovely,
Like the fleecy snow which in the sun beam
Melts. And she's here laid in her peaceful
Resting place: To wait the calling of her Lord.'
(King's Norton, MF747, of 1843)

Another interesting epitaph uses a metaphor to show the shortness of life:

'Like crowded forest trees you stand
And some are marked to fall
The axe will smite at God's command
And soon will level all.'
(Wootton Wawen, ME64, of 1864)

Very personal epitaphs are found on a few memorials at both churchyards, such as 'No more the foe can harm,'(King's Norton, MJ919, of 1918) which is on the memorial of a man who was buried in France whilst a prisoner of war. Individual personal messages show that choice was important to many people.

There are some excellent eighteenth and nineteenth century epitaphs which provide evidence about changing attitudes to death. The earliest epitaphs found are four line jingles. Often these were epitaphs which had been especially composed for memorials. Jingles remain a popular choice until the mid-nineteenth century when their use slowly fades as they are replaced by verses from scripture. Biblical epitaphs are found in use from the late eighteenth century and their use slowly increased until the late nineteenth century when they are by far the most popular choice. There is a large variety of epitaphs in both churchyards, with many of them occurring only once or twice in the yard. Texts were drawn from a wide variety of scriptural sources, many of which may have been taken from a mason's list, but others are more unusual and suggest that individual choice was possible. A few epitaphs were also taken from the Book of Common Prayer and quotations from hymns started to be used from the late nineteenth century.

As with the iconography, the age of mass production affects the words too.[30] Standardisation combines with stricter control by the church,[31] and epitaphs become shorter with less emotion by the late nineteenth century, accompanying stones that are often plain or identical. By the early twentieth century the majority of epitaphs are now one line, a perfect size to accompany the small headstones and kerbs which had become increasingly popular. The majority of twentieth century messages are shortened versions of scripture or hymns such as 'Peace, perfect peace,'[32] and 'In the midst of life we are in death.'[33] There are several references to sleep, and the tone of the messages is primarily soothing, with messages of peace and rest such as the popular 'At Rest,' 'Rest in peace' and 'Reunited'. The same theme is expressed in other definite messages from the period such as:

'Though now he bids us part
Reunion is sure and love is eternal.'
(King's Norton, MB61)

Inside the churches

The memorials inside the churches generally have very different epitaphs on them from those in the churchyard. The most popular iconography inside the churches is heraldry, with arms being a valued mark of status at both King's Norton and Wootton Wawen. Throughout the entire period of study the epitaphs complement this iconography with most of them being concerned with family history, occupation and virtues. The status of the people buried inside the church is emphasised by showing what they had achieved in life. This is why most of the epitaphs in the church are factual, describing the occupation, virtues and family history of the deceased. At King's Norton the memorial to Robert Mynors esquire describes his writings and profession as a surgeon (MCH2), and the memorial to John Southern first describes his work in mathematics and science and then goes on to list his personal virtues (MSA10). At Wootton Wawen the results are similar, with five of the Knight memorials giving only factual information about the lives of the deceased.

Also helping to emphasise status are epitaphs containing praise of the dead. At King's Norton the good works of

Sophia Gem and the patience of Harvey Gem are mentioned (MSA15, MSA18) and the memorial to the Taylor family praises Louisa, the wife of James Taylor, for her

'Exemplary piety,
Her conjugal, maternal and domestic virtues.'
(MNA10, OF 1822)

At Wootton Wawen many of the memorials praise the virtues of the deceased in their epitaphs, from the 'Integrity in high office' of George Henry Capewell Hughes (MSC16, of 1906) to the memorial to James Nugent which describes him as,

'A good Christian
An affectionate husband
A sincere friend
Requiescit in Pacem (sic).'
(MCH7, of 1762)

Personal virtues are also found on memorials commemorating vicars. Epitaphs list their virtues and what they had done for the parish in this role, such as on the memorial to Reverend Digby Henry Cotes Preedy at King's Norton from 1893:

'He endeared himself to all around him by
His kindness and earnest desire
For their spiritual and temporal welfare:
His devoted labours on
Behalf of the church and parish
During his ministry were recognized by
A Testimonial presented to his family
By a large number of friends and parishioners.'
(MCH1)

On the memorial to the Reverend James Hemming and family, the epitaph shows the importance of good works,

'Thy prayers and thine alms are come up for a
Memorial before God.'[34]
(MNA1)

At Wootton Wawen too it was also important to stress what the vicars had achieved in their other positions, such as the memorial to Daniel Gaches which records that he was a JP endowed 'With a force of intellect that was acute in analysis and firm and enduring in memory' (MCH1, of 1805). The memorial to Stanford Wolferstan lists his role as a vicar, but the epitaph is concerned with his other role of practising medicine:

'To souls and bodies too he med'
Cines gave
Like his great master willing
Both to save.'
(MCH4, of 1698)

There are a few religious epitaphs inside the churches at both King's Norton and Wootton Wawen which complement the iconography and show similar themes to those found outside in the churchyard. The earliest epitaphs emphasise the shortness of life and the closeness of death such as:

'My turn today, yours tomorrow.'
(Wootton Wawen, MCH12, of 1718)

The idea of the shortness of life is also found on an epitaph to Mary, wife of Lewis Bradley (MN11) at Wootton Wawen. These epitaphs complement the iconography of the period which was emphasising mortality with the use of symbols such as the skull. Also found during this period is RIP, which appears on three memorials at Wootton Wawen from the early eighteenth century, two of which have small crosses on them. All of these memorials appear to be Roman Catholics, particularly the memorial to Turbevil Needham, which is in Latin, whose

'..body lies here;
that His spirit however may in the day of the Lord obtain mercy,
Do you, O Catholic Traveller, pray that your fellow servant
May for ever Rest In Peace.'
(MCH5, of 1700)

The iconography inside the churches changes from representations of death to lighter and more hopeful images which show thoughts of victory over death and resurrection to eternal life with the use of urns, laurel branches and cherubs. Accompanying this is a change in the theme and tone of the epitaphs. Unlike earlier epitaphs which contain no reference to an afterlife, religious epitaphs of the nineteenth century become more positive and hopeful about salvation and resurrection. At King's Norton God's will and power are shown on two memorials, an idea which is accompanied by a reminder of the importance of faith for salvation:

'Be thou faithful unto death
And I will give thee a crown of life.'[35]
(MCH8, OF 1867)

Another three memorials show the importance of faith for salvation, and NA4 of 1915 shows the belief in resurrection:

'Because I live you shall live also.'[36]

At Wootton Wawen epitaphs of the nineteenth and early twentieth centuries also show more positive attitudes to death, with the theme of God's will, resurrection, and the importance of belief in salvation, such as on the memorial to Darwin Galton, 'At evening time it shall be light'[37] and 'Commit thy way unto the Lord and put thy trust in him and he shall bring it to pass.'[38] (SC10, of 1903)

There are also a couple of personal epitaphs at Wootton Wawen. One is to William Somervile, which was written by Somervile himself. The text from his epitaph on MSC20, of 1742, is translated on the memorial erected in the nave in 1898 to commemorate him:

'If you discover any virtue in me imitate it,
If you detect any failing shun it with your
Utmost strength. Remember that though young
You may be even now on the verge of death.

You know that you must die. Trust in Christ.'
(MN5)

Another personal epitaph was to the huntsman of William Somervile. This is on a tablet in the south aisle, which was erected in 1902, and is a copy of the original,[39] which has now faded from a headstone in the churchyard, commemorating Hoitt:

'Here Hoitt all his sports and labours past
Joins his loved master Somervile at last,
Together went they echoing fields to try,
Together now in silent quest they lie.
Servant and Lord, when once we yield our breath
Huntsman and poet are alike to death
Life's motley drama calls for powers, and men
Of different casts to fill its changeful scene
But all the merits that we justly prize,
Not in the part, but in the acting lies.
And, as the lyre, so may the huntsman's horn
Fame's trumpet rival, and his names adorn.'
(MSA2, erected 1902)

At Wootton Wawen the epitaph to John Phillips combines all of the elements found in epitaphs inside the churches, with the biographical detail in a long inscription about his life combined with a list of his virtues, and ends with the religious epitaph,

'Blessed are the dead which die in the Lord from henceforth Yea saith
the spirit that they may rest from
Their labours and their works do follow them.'[40]
(MSC5, of 1836)

[1] Matthew 24:44
[2] Isaiah 38:1
[3] Burial service, Book of Common Prayer
[4] Amos 4:12
[5] 1Corinthians 15:54
[6] John 11:25
[7] For more information about this see eds. P. Jupp and C. Gittings, *Death in England: An Illustrated History* (1999), Chapters 7, 8 and 9 and E. Royle, *Modern Britain: A Social History 1750-1997* (2nd edn, 1997), Chapter 6.
[8] Job 19:25
[9] 1Corinthians 15:22
[10] 1Peter 5:4
[11] Song of Solomon 2:17
[12] From a hymn entitled *Safe in the arms of Jesus*, written in 1870 by Frances Jane Alstyne
[13] Philippians 1:23
[14] Luke 18:16
[15] Ecclesiastes 12:7
[16] Revelations 14:13
[17] Matthew 11:28
[18] Romans 8:18
[19] Revelations 7:17
[20] From a hymn entitled *On the resurrection morning*, written in 1864 by Sabine Baring
[21] Matthew 6:10, 26:42
[22] Psalm 23:4
[23] Psalm 40:1
[24] Psalms 37:37 'Mark the perfect man and behold the upright, for the end of that man is peace'
[25] Hebrews 4:9
[26] Quoted by F. Burgess, *English Churchyard Memorials* (1963), pp. 32-33
[27] Proverbs 3:17
[28] Proverbs 12:4, 31:10
[29] Isaiah 40:11
[30] B. Bailey, *Churchyards of England and Wales* (1987), p. 152
[31] A. Wager, 'Three centuries of death: a study of the attitudes reflected in Gravestones in Shenstone (Staffs) Churchyard', *Transactions of the South Staffordshire Archaeological and Historical Society*, 19 (1979), pp. 47-55 (p. 54)
[32] From a hymn entitled *Peace, Perfect Peace, in this dark world of sin*, written by Edward Henry Bickersteth, 1875
[33] Burial Service, Book of Common Prayer
[34] Acts 10:4
[35] Revelation 2:10
[36] John 14:19
[37] Zechariah 14:7
[38] Psalms 37:5
[39] Cooper, *Wootton Wawen: Its History and Records* (1936), p. 73
[40] Revelation 14:13

Conclusion

There were two main objectives of the thesis: firstly, to see the extent to which a well preserved graveyard is, in isolation and with other sources, a reliable and representative database for local history, and, secondly, to examine whether important aspects of local communities living in significantly different socio-economic environments were reflected in the memorials.

The data obtained from the grave memorials for the investigation of age at death and time of year of death was compared with the parish registers to see whether they are historically reliable as a sample. The lack of surviving infant commemoration in the churchyards affected the statistics for age at death and month of death. The main discrepancy, therefore, between the data from the memorial stones and the parish registers is in the age group 0-9. In the churchyard this is the lowest age group recorded but in the parish registers this is the most frequently recorded age at death. Children have been found to be under-represented in similar studies elsewhere, and it is important to remember this when using memorials to study age at death.

Apart from the discrepancy in the age group 0-9 there were a few small differences between the results from the memorials and the parish registers, however, overall the comparison showed the memorials to be more accurate than expected thus indicating that grave memorials are a reliable source of information and are potentially useful for historical research. One important conclusion, however, is that many of those who are recorded in the registers as having being buried in the churchyards at King's Norton and Wootton Wawen – adults as much as pre-adults – may never have had a stone memorial. This conclusion emerges from the low percentages of memorials found there compared to the number of people known about from the registers, even in the early twentieth century.

Grave memorials are useful sources as they are 'documents in stone'.[1] They are primary sources recording a variety of information about people who died up to several hundred years ago. In isolation memorials are capable of giving information about a person in their entirety including name, age, sex, date of death and possibly birth, occupation, place of origin, status, family links and religious denomination. Genealogically, inscriptions are unique, a page in the story of someone's family of which there is only one copy.[2] Collectively the memorials studied here provide a portrait of the local communities concerned in the eighteenth, nineteenth and early twentieth centuries, giving records of men and women, local life and death, and religious feeling during successive stages of their society's history and evolution.[3]

The analysis of the memorials at King's Norton and Wootton Wawen shows that socio-economic changes are likely to be reflected in them. The memorials were analysed to investigate age at death. At both King's Norton and Wootton Wawen the people recorded from the churchyards appear to have been quite healthy in comparison to similar studies in more urban areas. Overall, life expectancy figures were higher than expected, with the ages 60 to 79 being the most frequently recorded age at death in both areas. The data from the grave memorials was mirrored in the parish registers except in the age group 0-9. Over the period from 1800 to 1940 the results from the grave memorials indicate that life expectancy increased at both King's Norton and Wootton Wawen and this was confirmed in the data from the parish registers. In very urban areas life expectancy is usually lower. For the majority of the period studied, however, King's Norton was still wholly rural, which explains the similarity in results from the two areas. The only difference is that the proportion of people living into their eighties was slightly greater at Wootton Wawen, and at King's Norton there were more deaths between the ages of 50 and 59. The differences between the two areas are confirmed in the parish registers and are possibly a result of the proximity of the parish of King's Norton to Birmingham.

The memorials were also useful for studying time of year of death. The results were again similar at King's Norton and Wootton Wawen, with most people dying in late winter and early spring and the fewest dying in summer. There are a few small discrepancies between the data from the memorials and the parish registers, but overall the results from the memorials are shown to be fairly reliable, with the results from the registers also showing that most deaths occurred in winter and spring and fewest in summer. It appears that the majority of people were affected by respiratory diseases and nutritional problems and were less susceptible to water and food borne diseases. The similarity between the two areas is not unusual because results throughout the country often show similar findings unless they are cities with very poor sanitation where deaths in summer would be higher.

The memorials from both churchyards indicate that for the people of King's Norton and Wootton Wawen it was not important to commemorate occupation or cause of death. The inscriptions on the memorials could however be used to investigate families. Commemorating lineage appears to be important to the people of both areas, with most of the stones referring to marital or family links or both. Several generations of a family are often found on one stone, and family links, such as people with different surnames, which may be difficult to see in parish registers alone can often be easier to identify using the inscriptions on the memorials and a plan of the churchyard.

The grave memorials at King's Norton and Wootton Wawen were not useful, however, for looking at family size. The results are potentially very inaccurate because of the probable lack of commemoration of children. As marital links appear to be more important to record, links between parents and children may be missed. Other links may be missed because older children may have moved away or be buried with their husband's family. No one else doing similar work has tried to use grave memorials to analyse family size, and so there was little that could be done comparatively.

The plans of the churchyards were used for a spatial analysis of the graves. At King's Norton the alignment of the memorials appears to have been affected by pathways and the boundary with the main road, and the areas closest to the church door and the main pathway to the church appear to have been affected by the need for space. The memorials at Wootton Wawen seem to have been affected by the position of the church doors and the pathways through the churchyard. The plans of the churchyards were also useful in analysing how the geography of the graveyard developed. At King's Norton place of origin does not appear to have been important in the geography of the graveyard. Instead, the plans indicate that the geography of the yard was heavily influenced by kin grouping, but was predominantly influenced by time. The earliest memorials were found in areas closest to the church in the south and east of the yard, and then extended outwards to areas surrounding the church. These areas were often the most popular places for burial, particularly the south side which is most often in the public view. For the east used to be thought of as the home of sunrise and hope, and the south as home of the warmth of midday.[4] Over time the northern side of the churchyard was used, and in the twentieth century memorials were predominantly found in the extensions to the churchyard on the west and northern sides.

At Wootton Wawen, place of origin appears to be more important in the geography of the graveyard, with the earliest Henley memorials found in section B and possibly another group between 1850 and 1899 in section E. The geography of the graveyard also seems to have been influenced by time, with the earliest memorials found in areas surrounding the church, but family links also appear to have been very important as family groups were found throughout the yard except in the twentieth century extension.

The memorials were used to try and identify who was buried inside the church. Social status was indicated by intramural burial which remained socially exclusive over the whole period studied. Memorials inside the churches show the importance of emphasising status by recording estates, titles and heraldry. Analysis of the memorials at Wootton Wawen indicates that those who were buried inside the church were people formally connected with the church, including those who owned estates which gave them rights to burial inside the church, even if they were Catholic, such as the Smith/Carington family. It appears to have been difficult for other people even to be commemorated inside the church with only people who had connections with those buried inside being commemorated before the prevention of burial in the late nineteenth century. After this date commemoration still appears to have been exclusive to people who had estates in the parish, and other people who were possibly important benefactors of the church.

At King's Norton there was a wider variety of people buried inside the church, but burial and commemoration inside remained socially exclusive for the entire period of study. The people who obtained burial were vicars and lords of the manors in the parish, as found at Wootton Wawen, but also the owners of other small estates, those who had risen in society mainly through commercial success and possibly benefactors of the church. As at Wootton Wawen it appears to have been difficult even to be commemorated inside the church, with the same types of people being found, such as those connected with the church, landed gentry, and those who had family connections with people who were buried inside the church. After the prevention of intramural burial there were also memorials erected inside the church to commemorate those who had died during war. Social status was also indicated outside in both of the churchyards by the size and location of the memorials. Documentary evidence showed the families recorded on these memorials to be of local importance.

The type and shape of the stones and their iconography and epitaphs provides a wealth of information. Both churchyards show the influence of architectural fashions in the type and shape of the stones, such as in moving from the simplicity of the classical revival to the pointed and three-dimensional crosses of the gothic revival. In both churchyards the memorials start to become smaller in the twentieth century, but at King's Norton the standardisation of stones is clearly marked with rows and rows of kerbs, Celtic crosses, rocks and book shapes. The people of Wootton Wawen were much slower in following this trend.

In both churchyards there are plain memorials, but there are also many people who appear to use the memorials to express religious and social feelings. Changes in attitudes to death are coupled with architectural fashions and are shown in the iconography on the memorials. The earliest stones at Wootton Wawen show the obsession with time and death, using the deaths-head and symbols of mortality. From this a more hopeful period develops at both churchyards. The influence of the Baroque and roccoco styles is combined with thoughts of resurrection and salvation in gentler images such as cherubs. The theme of hope and belief in salvation then continues with the classical revival, which introduces new images such as the urn, crown, trumpets, torches and doves. The Gothic revival influences architecture and is used at a time of religious seriousness, with traditional Christian symbols such as the cross and IHS. At Wootton Wawen traditional Christian symbols are used alongside neo-classical ones, with the cross appearing early and featuring heavily. This is probably because Wootton Wawen was an important centre of Roman Catholicism which included the Smith/Carrington family who were lords of the manor.[5] These people appear to have considered it important to show their religion. The theme of resurrection and remembrance is popular in both yards from the mid-nineteenth century, with the use of symbols such as flowers and the sickle. Memorials inside the churches show similar symbols to those in the churchyard, with the exception of heraldry. This was rare outside in the churchyard but was a popular choice inside the church, helping to show status.

Much of the inspiration for the changes in shape and iconography is probably derived from changes in architectural fashions and emblem and pattern books. Stonemasons learnt about these new trends and introduced them to the people of the area. Analysis of the stonemasons found on memorials at both churchyards was done as far as was possible. Few names were found on memorials before the mid nineteenth century, and so some of the excellent earlier work had no stonemason named on it. Analysis after this date in both areas shows several local[6] stonemasons whose work follows the influence of fashions in architecture and pattern books.

Several of the nonconformists and Roman Catholics who were indicated in the parish registers were found commemorated on memorial stones in the churchyards. None of these stones used different iconography from Anglican stones of the same period. As the sample was small perhaps more work could be done on this in areas where nonconformists can be easily identified from the burial registers.

The memorials of family groups were analysed to see if they were similar. The iconography shows that although architectural trends and changes in attitudes to death were influential on iconography, choice was very important. As shown in the geography of the yard there were several families at King's Norton and particularly at Wootton Wawen who wanted to be together in death as well as life. As well as having their stones grouped together in the yard several of the family groups also have identical stones.

The iconography at King's Norton and Wootton Wawen was compared to that from the memorials recorded in the yard of the Roman Catholic church of St Joseph's Nechells, and in those at St Margaret's, Ward End, St Philip's and St Paul's in Birmingham, and Key Hill and Warstone Lane cemeteries. This was done so as to discover if people from areas which were wholly urban for the entire period of study, were quicker to learn about and utilize trends in fashion. The results from the comparison show that neither King's Norton nor Wootton Wawen was particularly slow in following the fashions, with new designs being found in these churchyards at the same time as in those in the city of Birmingham. The more rural Wootton Wawen even uses some of the symbols earlier than King's Norton. The results from studying memorials in the city centre show that even with mass production and standardization choice can still be important. There are individual designs amongst the masses of uniform stones, and where religion is important this heavily influences the design of the monument. The finest work in all of the churchyards is found before the mid-nineteenth century, after which large firms start to standardize their designs and individual craftsmanship becomes a rarity.

It is easy to see why iconography is most frequently written about because it is concerned not just with the history of the local community but with the history of

'folk art'[7] and attitudes to death. Individual stones can be masterpieces of artistic craftsmanship. Excellent iconography is not only found in urban churchyards. There are some visually stunning memorials at both King's Norton and Wootton Wawen.

The epitaphs on the memorials contain valuable insights into attitudes to death. The theme and tone of the epitaphs accompany changes in the iconography, moving from the early expressions of fear and warning about death and God's wrath, to messages with a lighter tone, which are at first hesitant and hopeful when talking about salvation, heaven and the afterlife, but which become more definite from the mid-nineteenth century onwards. Hiding the reality of death is found on several memorials where metaphors are used to describe the deceased. Epitaphs show the increased expression of sentiment and become more personal over the period studied with messages of remembrance and grief being popular in the late nineteenth and early twentieth centuries.

It is important to consider the extent to which the iconography and epitaphs show genuinely personal expressions of people's emotions and their attitudes to death over time, or whether these were just stock items chosen from a stonemason's or undertaker's list. Do trends in iconography and epitaphs show the real feelings of the people or were they just following fashion? An important lesson to be learnt from this study is that there are general trends in the iconography and epitaphs, which result from fashions in architecture and changes in religious feeling. The study of iconography showed however that people did not always follow the new trends. Commemorating the death of a person was an important matter, and this is reflected in all aspects of the memorial, particularly the iconography and epitaphs. Individual choice was possible, and where religion was important to the people it heavily influenced the design of the memorial. This was most clearly shown in the iconography at the Roman Catholic Church of St Joseph's, Nechells, which favoured biblical and Christian symbols at a time when they were in little use in other city centre yards. The epitaphs also showed that people followed new trends at their own pace as epitaphs with very different tones were found to be in use during the same period. Even where the themes of the iconography and epitaphs were similar, a wide variety of different stones and epitaphs were found in both churchyards. There were very few stones that had identical iconography or epitaphs on them, which may also indicate that personal selection was possible and that we are hearing genuine expressions of attitudes to death within conventional parameters set by the funerary profession.

Several lessons can be learnt from the work done at King's Norton and Wootton Wawen. It is important not to try to be too quick when recording grave memorials, as misreading numbers and words can be easy particularly if the inscription on the stone is fading. On more than one occasion my original recording of the inscription was found to be incorrect as I had mistaken numbers such as 3 and 8, or 5 and 6. This can be remedied by a very careful rereading of the whole stone after the initial recording, and sometimes it can help to feel the shape of the incised letters when unsure about them. It is also important to return to some memorials more than once to try and decipher a partly legible stone. Any doubtful readings can often be cleared up by a comparison of the recording with the parish registers. When recording memorials it is also necessary to look for stones everywhere in the churchyards, as full stones or parts of memorials can be propped up anywhere, and can also be found hiding in pavements, in walls, and in the middle of bushes.

The comparative study has shown the wealth of information that can be found from grave memorials. Even with the work already completed, there is still much analysis that could be done on the churchyards at King's Norton and Wootton Wawen, particularly on geology of the stones and the development of lettering. There is still regional bias in work on funerary practices towards London and the south-east, and so more yards need to be recorded from other areas and comparisons need to be made between rural and urban graveyards in areas where the latter are much better preserved than was found to be the case in Birmingham. More generally there is still much work to be done in this field, considering that churchyards are estimated as taking up over 25,000 acres of land.[8] Hundreds of yards have been claimed to be recorded when in fact only a genealogy has been compiled.[9] Graveyards are a wasting historical asset. There are thousands of churchyards which still need to be recorded, and each memorial only has a limited natural lifespan, made shorter by man-made destruction and the threat of clearance. Stones are destroyed at an alarming rate, possibly because there is no understanding of their historical value.[10] Destruction of churchyards means loss of a place not only of memories and commemoration of loved ones but of vital information about the past and the people inhabiting it.

Memorial stones are the uppermost layer of an archaeological site and directly relate to the graves below.[11] They contain a wealth of information, and in showing the work of local men are a legacy of the skills of our ancestors.[12] Grave memorials are part of the history of a community, containing information about the lives of ordinary people and historical data which has a variety of applications, biographical, genealogical, demographic, socio-economic, and they can inform us about attitudes to life, death and God.[13] Epitaphs are one of the richest yet most neglected sources of information on the lives and customs of our ancestors.[14] They provide a valuable insight into social and family history. Epitaphs can inform us about the minutiae of life, which in the absence of documents would remain forever unknown.[15] Gravestones show people in their entirety, and no other source contains this variety of information. Some of this information can be found in parish registers but the comparison of the data from the memorials with the registers has shown that the grave memorials are a reliable historical source which could be used in areas where there are no alternative sources available. Graveyard memorials can also provide unique evidence which cannot be found in the parish registers, such as in the iconography and the epitaphs which are possibly the most valuable aspect of graveyard study,[16] providing unique evidence of attitudes to death and changes in religious feeling. Parish registers are also devoid of the sentiment which is found in the inscription on the memorial stones.

There are regional variations and differences between individual graveyards. Each churchyard is unique, a 'product of men, the landscape and the effects of time.'[17] Because of this some churchyards may show unreliable results. This will not be known until the stones are recorded and the results analysed. Even if this is the case the graveyard is as much a part of the local history as the church and will usually contain monuments which, apart from their role as irreplaceable historical documents, have an important aesthetic value.[18] Even after the inscription has faded many are still works of art in their own right and are worthy of preservation.[19] Grave memorials are an important body of historical evidence. They need to be at least recorded and, where possible, preserved before they are lost forever.

[1] P. A. Rahtz, 'The Archaeology of the Churchyard', in ed. P. Addyman and R. Morris, *The Archaeological Study of Churches*, Council for British Archaeology Research Report 13 (1976), p. 42, cited hereafter as Rahtz, 'Archaeology of the Churchyard'

[2] J. L. Rayment, *Notes on the Recording of Monumental Inscriptions* (1981), p. 3

[3] B. Bailey, *Churchyards of England and Wales* (1987), p. 185, cited hereafter as Bailey, *Churchyards*

[4] W. Johnson, *Byways in British Archaeology* (1912), pp. 328-330

[5] ed. W. Page, The Victoria History of the Counties of England, *Warwickshire, Volume II* (1965), pp. 45-46

[6] These were stonemasons from the parish such as Locker of King's Norton and Kings Heath at King's Norton and Keen of Henley, at Wootton Wawen.

[7] D. Neave and V. Heron, 'Slate Headstones and their engravers', *The Local Historian* 8.6 (1969), pp. 213-217 (p. 217)

[8] Bailey, *Churchyards*, p. 19

[9] W. Rodwell, *The Archaeology of the English Church* (1981), p. 166

[10] Rahtz, 'Archaeology of the Churchyard', p. 43

[11] *Ibid*. p. 42

[12] H. Lees, *English Churchyard Memorials* (2000), p. 11, cited hereafter as Lees, *Memorials*

[13] J. Jones, 'The Grave memorials of the church of St Mary, Deerhurst, Gloucestershire' (University of Birmingham, unpublished BA dissertation, 1972), p. 55

[14] K. Lindley, *Of Graves and Epitaphs* (1965), p. 147, cited hereafter as Lindley, *Graves*

[15] F. Burgess, *English Churchyard Memorials* (1963), p. 220

[16] P. A. Rahtz, 'Wroxeter Churchyard 1974', *West Midlands Archaeological News Sheet*, 17 (1974), pp. 28-31 (p. 31)

[17] Lindley, *Graves*, p. 18

[18] I. Shorters, 'A study of the grave memorials of Holy Trinity Church, Baswich, Staffordshire' (University of Birmingham, unpublished BA dissertation, 2000), p. 74

[19] Lees, *Memorials*, p. 142

Appendix 1: Burial inside the churches at Wootton Wawen and King's Norton

There were several memorials inside the churches at both King's Norton and Wootton Wawen which were not included in the analysis in Chapter 2 as they were erected earlier than the stones in the churchyard. These memorials will be examined here along with some of the families not discussed in detail during the Chapter.

Wootton Wawen:

The earliest memorials commemorate people who were buried inside the church for similar reasons to those discussed in Chapter 2. Some of the memorials show people who had burial rights inside the church. John Aylesbury, as owner of Edstone, had burial rights on the south side of the chapel.[1] He is commemorated on SC28. Another of the earliest memorials commemorates William Somervile (MSC3), who also had burial rights inside the church because of his ownership of Edstone. The memorial to William who died in 1676 is the earliest of the Somervile[2] memorials.

Two of the other early memorials commemorate George Dunscombe (SC24), Vicar of Wootton Wawen from 1642-1652, who gave chained books to the church[3] and Mary Whittel, wife of John Whittel of Bearley (SC32, of 1603). There is no indication of why Mary was buried inside the church and the memorial shows no links with any other memorials. She may possibly have been an important benefactor of the church.

The Knight family

Another of the earliest memorials inside the church commemorates a member of the Knight family. The memorial is dated 1681 and commemorates John Knight of Barrells. The story of the Knight family shows an extraordinary rise from a sub-manor to a peerage. The estate of Barrells was purchased by Robert Knight, of a cadet branch of the Knight family of Barrells, in 1730. He also acquired the manor of Edstone in 1745.[4] The way was paved for Robert Knight (who became Baron Luxborough in 1745 and Earl of Catherlough in 1763), by the fortune of his father who was cashier of the South Sea Company.[5] He commemorates him on one of the six memorials he erected to his family in the South Chapel.

The Harewell/Smith/Carington family

Four of the earliest memorials in the church commemorate members of the Harewell/Smith/Carington family. The Harewell/Smith/Carington family were buried inside the church because their ownership of estates gave them the right. Probably the oldest memorial in the church is an altar tomb with a recumbent effigy of the early fifteenth century and shields with the Harewell arms on them (MCH6). This is most probably the tomb of John Harewell who died in 1428. The manor of the Harewell family[6] (later known as the manor of Lucies) had descended to John in 1390 through his father Roger

Harewell and the Harewells were increasing their lands and possessions in other places besides Wootton, so that they were ranked highly amongst the gentry of the shire.[7] John Harewell, esquire, died in 1505, and with his wife Ann is commemorated on an altar tomb in the chancel, which shows shields displaying the family arms (MCH2).

Another family descendant, Lady Agnes died in 1562 and was buried in the Chapel of Wootton Wawen where a tablet affixed to the north wall (SC17) marks her resting place. Francis Carrington is commemorated on SC 18, a grand renaissance tomb with the family arms on. His marriage brought the estates of Ashby Folville and other lands to the Smith family and he added considerably to his possessions. Francis was the last high sole high sheriff of the two counties of Warwick and Leicester.

The Smith-Caringtons are descendants of the Harewell family and therefore had rights on the north side of the chapel where the monuments to Agnes and Francis are found. More often than not, however, the Smith family resided and were buried at their other estate at Ashby Folville. A flat stone in the chancel commemorates the Honourable Frances Carrington who died in 1698, wife of Charles Carrington, (later the third Viscount Carington) who died in 1706, one of the heirs of Wootton manor. The latest memorial to this family is SC22 in the south chapel, a flat stone in front of the altar step next to the north wall. This commemorates Francis Carington who only had possession of the estates for one year before his death in 1749.

Phillips/Galton family

As an owner of the manor of Edstone John Phillips had burial rights inside the church. He is commemorated on SC5, a tablet on the south wall of the chapel. John Phillips, esquire, was born in Droitwich, became a barrister, and in 1803 was high sheriff of Worcester. He was buried in the family vault in the chapel and his burial is marked by a flat stone (SC27). His wife, lady of the manor for 22 years, is commemorated on SC9, a tablet on the south wall. Other memorials linked to the Phillips family are SC 7 and 8, which commemorate their eldest daughter Mary Elisabeth and her son John Samuel Phillips. Mary was the first wife of Darwin Galton, JP DL, an active magistrate, who also owned the manor of Henley and is commemorated on SC10; and his second wife is commemorated on SC6.

King's Norton:

As with the memorials at Wootton Wawen the earliest memorials at King's Norton emphasise the exclusivity of burial inside the church. On the north side of the tower is the earliest monument found in the church (MT3) This is an altar-tomb which originally stood in the south-east corner of the north aisle. The tomb commemorates Humfrie Littelton of Grovelry and his wife Martha who died in 1588. Martha was the daughter of Robert Gower, who was in possession of the manor of Colmers in King's Norton. Humfrie is not actually buried in the church, he outlived his wife by 36 years and had the monument erected during that period. He was finally laid to rest at Naunton Beauchamp near Pershore.[8]

On the south side of the tower is a seventeenth century altar tomb (MT2), which was originally in the chancel next to the altar. The tomb has shields on it displaying heraldry and this together with the inscription indicates the importance of the deceased. It commemorates Sir Richard Grevis, Knight, who held the manor of Moseley Hall and estate, and his wife Dame Ann. Sir Richard died in 1632, a wealthy landowner with other large estates in Solihull, Castle Bromwich and Sutton.[9] More unusual inside the church at King's Norton is a very small stone in the north aisle commemorating William Greves who was 'slaine' in 1605 (MNA8). Greves was a tax collector who was murdered for his takings while living alone in his cottage on Parson's Hill.[10]

The Pountney family

Four memorials in the church commemorate members of the family who died between 1804 and 1879. The Pountney family were a wealthy local family who were owners of an estate in the parish. There are no titles in their inscriptions but references to Monyhull Hall, which descended through John, Richard and Humphrey Pountney until it was sold in 1864.[11] Humphrey died in 1852 and is recorded on Memorial C7. Other family members commemorated in the church are Richard Pountney of Rostrevoir House, Green Lanes, Aston (MSA9) and Thomas Pountney of Millpool Hill (SA12). It is difficult to tell which of the Pountney family were buried inside the church as it states on MSA9 that Richard was buried in the family vault under the vestry but all of the Pountney family who are commemorated inside the church are also recorded on the family tomb outside.

---

[1] In W. Cooper, *Wootton Wawen: Its History and Records* (1936), Cooper gives an account of church rights and responsibilities on pages 91 to 92, and the owners of Edstone Hall on pages 74-76

[2] The Somervile family are discussed in detail in Chapter 2, pp. 91-96

[3] W. Cooper, *Wootton Wawen: Its History and Records* (1936), pp. 102 and 121, cited hereafter as Cooper, *Wootton Wawen*

[4] Robert Knight is discussed in Chapter 2, p. 97

[5] S. Bassett, *The Wootton Wawen Project: Report Number 6* (1988), p. 14

[6] Cooper, *Wootton Wawen* pp. 13-37

[7] *Ibid.* p. 17

[8] H. Goodger, *King's Norton* (1990), p. 54, cited hereafter as Goodger, *King's Norton*

[9] *Ibid.* p. 15

[10] *Ibid.* p. 55

[11] *Ibid.* p. 23

Appendix 2: Iconography found on the earliest memorials inside the churches at King's Norton and Wootton Wawen

There are some excellent early monuments inside the churches at both King's Norton and Wootton Wawen.[1] As with the later memorials which were discussed in Chapter 3, the earliest monuments inside the churches show the influence of architectural fashions and religious feeling. Again showing family pride and status was important with heraldry being the most predominant iconography on the earliest memorials.

Effigies are found on monuments at both King's Norton and Wootton Wawen. In the twelfth century effigies showed the deceased alive and standing but slowly the strictly recumbent effigy became popular and by about 1350 the standard late medieval form was achieved which showed the deceased as recumbent with legs straight and hands clasped together in prayer.[2] An example of this style of effigy is shown at Wootton Wawen where in the chancel against the north wall there stands a marble altar tomb with the alabaster effigy of a man in full plate armour (MCH6, Figure 63). The monument dates from the early fifteenth century and most probably commemorates John Harewell who died in 1428. His head rests on a helm, his feet rest on a long-eared dog and the sides of the tomb have the family arms on them. Much of the base of the tomb has been restored.

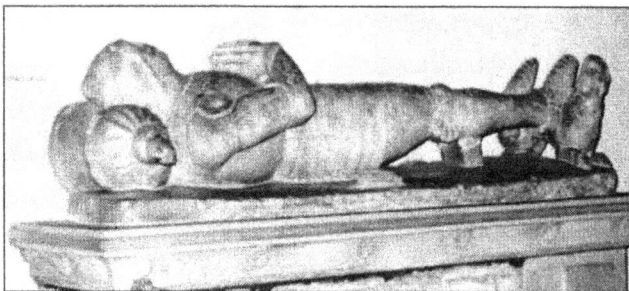

Figure 63. Wootton Wawen: an example of a strictly recumbent effigy (MCH6, probably of 1428)

The family arms are also shown on another Harewell memorial in the chancel which dates from 1505 (MCH2) and commemorates the great-grandson of John Harewell and his wife and children.[3] This is an altar tomb and on the top slab are the brass effigies of John Harewell, died 1505, and his wife Lady Anne. He is in full armour and she is in headdress and gown. The hands of both figures are joined in prayer. Below the brass effigies are the figures of their five sons and five daughters who are depicted as standing with their hands raised in prayer.

The deceased are shown in engravings on sixteenth century memorial at King's Norton. On the north side of the tower an altar tomb of 1588 commemorates Humphrey Littelton of Grovelry and his wife (MT3, Figure 64). Their two life-size figures are engraved on a flat alabaster slab with the man shown in armour with his head on a helmet and the woman in period dress with her head on a cushion.[4] Both figures have their hands clasped together in a position of prayer. An interesting feature of this tomb is a relief carving of an infant on the side of the memorial which indicates the death of a child and reminds us of the grim aspect of death. This is a chrysom child, wrapped in a chrysom cloth which is a sheet used to wrap or swaddle an infant for the service of baptism.

Figure 64. King's Norton: an example of a chrysom child on the Littelton memorial (MT3, of 1588)

The recumbent style of effigy remained the normal portrayal until the sixteenth century. The Renaissance encouraged depiction of the dead as they were in life and therefore recumbent effigies were raised up from death and were placed in standing, kneeling and reclining positions.[5] At King's Norton in the tower a recess in the wall houses two figures kneeling in prayer (MT4, Figure 65). The couple are dressed in seventeenth century costume[6] but there is no inscription and no date on the memorial. Monuments with figures kneeling in prayer were popular on smaller wall memorials during this period, particularly for couples who were often depicted face to face over a prayer desk.[7]

Figure 65. King's Norton: an example of kneeling effigies (MT4)

An excellent example of a reclining effigy is found at Wootton Wawen in the south chapel (MSC18, Figure 66). This is a chest tomb with a canopy over the top. The memorial commemorates Francis Smith who died in 1605, and shows him in armour which according to Cooper is typical of the earlier part of Queen Elizabeth's reign.[8] Family arms are on the head and base of the memorial and these are combined with emblems of mortality, carved in relief, which were popular during this period. These symbols of mortality hang on either side of the top-inscription and include bones, hour glass, scythe, spade and mattock.

Figure 66. Wootton Wawen: the reclining effigy of Francis Smith (MSC18)

The recumbent effigy did not totally disappear from use in church monuments, however, and a later example of one is shown at King's Norton. The Grevis tomb (MT2, Figure 67) is a seventeenth century altar tomb sculpted from alabaster with the recumbent figures of Richard Grevis of Moseley and Ann, his wife. The attention to detail is shown in the clothes of the figures who are shown in the dress and armour of the period. On a slab above are the kneeling effigies of their four sons and four daughters dressed in detailed clothes of the period.[9] The grouping of effigies on monuments had become increasingly popular from the late sixteenth century when it was common for the whole family to be depicted on the memorial. The husband and wife were often full size-effigies as they are in this example, with the children kneeling in a row on its front. More unusual was for the children to be placed on the backplate as they are here.[10] At the highest point of the memorial are the arms of the family and arms are also shown on the base of the tomb.

Figure 67. King's Norton: an example of a seventeenth century altar tomb with recumbent effigies (MT2)

Apart from the larger monuments there are a few early examples of hanging wall monuments at Wootton Wawen. Heraldry is again popular, appearing alone on the flat stone commemorating John Knight of Barrells (SC30, of 1681) and on the wall monument to William Somervile who died in 1676. The decorative frame is an excellent example of the influence of the baroque period on memorials (SC3, Figure 68).

Figure 68. Wootton Wawen: an example of the influence of the baroque in the decoration of the frame (SC3, of 1676)

67

[1] For more detail on the early monuments inside the churches see W. Cooper, *Wootton Wawen: Its History and Records* (1936), pp. 108-119, and H. Goodger, *King's Norton* (1990), pp. 52-56

[2] B. Kemp, *Church Monuments* (1985), pp. 15-16, cited hereafter as Kemp, *Monuments*

[3] W. Cooper, *Wootton Wawen: Its History and Records* (1936), p. 108, cited hereafter as Cooper, *Wootton Wawen*

[4] ed. J. W. Willis-Bund, The Victoria History of the Counties of England, *Worcestershire, Volume III* (1913), p. 189, cited hereafter as VCH, *Worcs*, III

[5] K. Esdaile, *English Monumental Sculpture Since the Renaissance* (1927), p. 53

[6] VCH, *Worcs*, III, p. 189

[7] Kemp, *Monuments*, p. 16

[8] Cooper, *Wootton Wawen*, p. 112

[9] VCH, *Worcs*, III, p. 189

[10] Kemp, *Monuments*, pp. 19-21

BIBLIOGRAPHY

Primary sources:

King's Norton parish registers
Birmingham Central Library: *Registers of the Church of St. Nicholas, King's Norton, Worcestershire. Part two: baptisms and burial 1792-1844, marriages 1754-1837* (1981)
Birmingham Central Library: *Registers of the Church of St. Nicholas, King's Norton, Worcestershire. Part three: marriages 1546-1754, burials 1546-1791* (1983)
Birmingham Central Library, History and Local Studies Department, EP4/2/4/1 (King's Norton Burials 1813-1844)
Birmingham Central Library, History and Local Studies Department, EP4/2/4/2 (King's Norton Burials 1844-1870)
Birmingham Central Library, History and Local Studies Department, EP4/2/4/3 (King's Norton Burials 1870-1894)
Birmingham Central Library, History and Local Studies Department, EP4/2/4/4 (King's Norton Burials 1894-1908)
Birmingham Central Library, History and Local Studies Department, EP4/2/4/5 (King's Norton Burials 1908-1922)
Birmingham Central Library, History and Local Studies Department, EP4/2/4/6 (King's Norton Burials 1922-1944)

Wootton Wawen parish registers
Warwickshire County Record Office, DR195/3 (Wootton Wawen Baptisms, Marriages and Burials 1700-1723)
Warwickshire County Record Office, DR195/4 (Wootton Wawen Baptisms, Marriages and Burials 1723-1812)
Warwickshire County Record Office, DR195/13 (Wootton Wawen Baptisms, Marriages and Burials 1813-1869)
Warwickshire County Record Office, DR740/3 (Wootton Wawen Baptisms, Marriages and Burial 1869-1979)

Bishop's Transcripts (1790-1811)
Worcester Record Office, references b736, BA2015/346 to b736 BA2015/367

Books:

B. Bailey, *Churchyards of England and Wales* (London, 1987)
S. M. Barnard, *To Prove I'm Not Forgot: Living and Dying in a Victorian City* (Manchester University Press, 1990)
S. Bassett, *The Wootton Wawen Project: Report Number 2* (1984)
S. Bassett, *The Wootton Wawen Project: Report Number 3* (1985)
S. Bassett, *The Wootton Wawen Project: Report Number 4* (1986)
S. Bassett, *The Wootton Wawen Project: Report Number 5* (1987)
S. Bassett, *The Wootton Wawen Project: Report Number 6* (1988)
F. Bédarida, *A Social History of England 1851-1990* (2nd edn., London, 1991)
A. Briggs, *History of Birmingham. Volume II. Borough and City, 1865-1938* (Oxford University Press, 1952)
C. Brooks, *Mortal Remains: The History and Present State of the Victorian and Edwardian Cemetery* (London, 1989)
F. Burgess, *English Churchyard Memorials* (London, 1963)
W. Cooper, *Wootton Wawen: Its History and Records* (Leeds, 1936)
G. Cope, ed., *Dying Death and Disposal* (London, 1970)
M. Cox, ed., *Grave Concerns. Death and Burial in England 1700-1850* (Council for British Archaeology, Research Report 113, 1998)
J. S. Curl, *The Victorian Celebration of Death* (London, 1972)
L. Dunkling and W. Gosling, *Everyman's Dictionary of First Names* (3rd edn., London, 1991)
K. A. Esdaile, *English Monumental Sculpture Since the Renaissance* (London, 1927)
K. A. Esdaile, *English Church Monuments, 1510 to 1840* (London, 1946)
E. J. Evans, *The Forging of the Modern State: Early Industrial Britain 1783-1870* (Foundations of Modern Britain, Longman, 1983)
J. Finch, *Church Monuments in Norfolk Before 1850: An Archaeology of Commemoration* (British Archaeological Reports, British Series 317, 2000)
R. Fletcher, *The Akenham Burial Case* (London, 1974)
C. Gill, *History of Birmingham. Volume 1. Manor and Borough to 1865* (Oxford University Press, 1952)
C. Gittings, *Death, Burial and the Individual in Early Modern England* (London, 1984)
H. Goodger, *King's Norton* (Warwickshire, 1990)
J. E. B. Gover, A. Mawer, and F. M. Stenton in collaboration with F. T. S. Houghton, *The Place-Names of Warwickshire* (English Place Names Society, vol. XIII, Cambridge University Press, 1936)
M. Green, ed., *Images of England: King's Heath* (Birmingham City Council, Department of Leisure and Community Services, 1998)
J. Harris, *Private Lives, Public Spirit: A Social History of Britain 1870-1914* (Oxford University Press, 1993)
R. Houlbrooke, ed., *Death, Ritual and Bereavement* (London, 1989)
W. Johnson, *Byways in British Archaeology* (Cambridge University Press, 1912)
J. Jones, *How to Record Graveyards* (2nd edn., Council For British Archaeology, 1979)
P. C. Jupp and C. Gittings, eds., *Death in England: An Illustrated History* (Manchester University Press, 1999)
P. C. Jupp and G. Howarth, eds., *The Changing Face of Death: Historical Accounts of Death and Disposal* (London, 1997)
B. Kemp, *English Church Monuments* (London, 1980)
B. Kemp, *Church Monuments* (Shire Publications Ltd, Buckinghamshire, 1985)
P. Laslett, *The World We Have Lost: Further Explored* (3rd edn., Cambridge University Press, 1983)
H. Lees, *English Churchyard Memorials* (Stroud, 2000)
K. Lindley, *Of Graves and Epitaphs* (London, 1965)
J. Litten, *The English Way of Death. The Common Funeral since 1450* (London, 1991)
Longman Concise English Dictionary (1985)
A. Mawer and F. M. Stenton, in collaboration with F. T. S. Houghton, *The Place Names of Worcestershire* (English Place Name Society, vol. IV, Cambridge University Press, 1927)
J. McKenna, *In the Midst of Life: a history of the Burial Grounds of Birmingham* (Birmingham Library Series, 1992)
R. Millward and A. Robinson, *The West Midlands* (London, 1971)
J. Mitford, *The American Way of Death* (USA, 1963)
T. Molleson and M. Cox, *The Spitalfields Project. Volume 2: Anthropology* (Council for British Archaeology, Research Report 86, 1993)
J. Morley, *Death, Heaven and the Victorians* (London, 1971)
H. Mytum, *Recording and Analysing Graveyards* (Council for British Archaeology, 2000)
W. Page, ed., *The Victoria History of the Counties of England: Warwickshire, Volume II*, (1965)
D. Pickering, *The Penguin Dictionary of First Names* (London, 1999)
R. Porter, *English Society in the Eighteenth Century* (London, 1982)
R. Porter, ed., *Disease, Medicine and Society in England, 1550-1860* (Studies in Economic and Social History, 2nd edn., Basingstoke, 1993)
B. S. Puckle, *Funeral Customs: Their Origin and Development* (London, 1926)
J. L. Rayment, *Notes on the Recording of Monumental Inscriptions* (3rd edn., 1981)
J. Reeve and M. Adams, *The Spitalfields Project. Volume 1: The Archaeology* (Council for British Archaeology, Research Report 85, 1993)
R. Richardson, *Death, Dissection and the Destitute* (London, 1987)
W. Rodwell, *The Archaeology of the English Church* (1981)
W. J. Rodwell and K. A. Rodwell, *Rivenhall: Investigations of a Villa, Church and Village, 1950-1977* (Council for British Archaeology, Research Report 55, 1986)
W. J. Rodwell and K. A. Rodwell, *Rivenhall: Investigations of a Villa, Church and Village, 1950-1977. Volume 2* (Council for British Archaeology, Research Report 80, 1993)
E. Royle, *Modern Britain. A Social History 1750-1997* (2nd edn., London 1997)
W. D. Rubinstein, *Britain's Century: A Political and Social History 1815-1905* (London, 1998)
L. F. Salzman, ed., *The Victoria History of the Counties of England: Warwick, Volume III, Barlichway Hundred* (1945)
V. Skipp, *A History of Greater Birmingham: Down to 1830* (Birmingham, 1980)
V. Skipp, *The Making of Victorian Birmingham* (Birmingham, 1983)
T. Slater, *A History of Warwickshire* (Sussex, 1997)
D. J. Steel, ed., *National Index of Parish Registers. Volume 1. Sources of Births, Marriages and Deaths before 1837* (London, 1968)
W. B. Stephens, ed., *The Victoria History of the Counties of England: Warwick, Volume VII: The City of Birmingham* (1964)

W. E. Tate, *The Parish Chest: A Study of the Records of Parochial Administration in England* (3rd edn., 1969)

F. M. L. Thompson, ed., *The Cambridge Social History of Britain 1750-1950. Volume 2: People and their Environment* (Cambridge University Press, 1990)

F. M. L. Thompson, ed., *The Cambridge Social History of Britain 1750-1950. Volume 3: Social Agencies and Institutions* (Cambridge University Press, 1990)

C. Upton, *A History of Birmingham* (Sussex, 1993)

J. E. Vaughan, *The Parish Church and Ancient Grammar School of King's Norton* (6th edn., Gloucester, 1971)

W. T. Vincent, *In Search of Gravestones Old and Curious* (1896)

L. Weaver, *Memorials and Monuments* (London, 1915)

J. W. Willis-Bund, ed., *The Victoria History of the Counties of England: Worcestershire, Volume III* (1913)

E. G. Withycombe, *The Oxford Dictionary of English Christian Names* (3rd edn., Oxford University Press, 1977)

A. Wood, *Nineteenth Century Britain, 1815-1914* (Harlow, 1982)

E. A. Wrigley, ed., *An Introduction to English Historical Demography: From the Sixteenth to the Nineteenth Century* (London, 1966)

E. A. Wrigley and R. S. Schofield, *The Population History of England, 1541-1871. A Reconstruction* (London, 1981)

Articles:

E. Dethlefsen and J. Deetz, 'Death's heads, cherubs and willow trees: experimental archaeology in colonial cemeteries', *American Antiquity*, 31 (1966), pp.502-510

J. Deetz and E. Dethlefsen, 'Some social aspects of New England colonial art', *American Antiquity*, 36 (1971), no 3, part 2, pp.30-38

J. Dove, 'A comparison of gravestones in two country churchyards', *Proceedings of the Geologist's Association, 103* (1992), pp. 143-154

D. Neave and V. Heron, 'Slate headstones and their engravers', *The Local Historian*, 8.6 (1969), pp.213-217

P. A. Rahtz, 'Wroxeter Churchyard 1974', *West Midlands Archaeological News Sheet*, 17 (1974), pp.28-31

P. A. Rahtz, 'The archaeology of the churchyard' in ed. P. Addyman and R. Morris, *The Archaeological Study of Churches*, (Council For British Archaeology, Research Report 13, 1976), pp.41-45

P. Rahtz, 'Wharram Percy memorial stones: an anthropological view from Mars' in ed. D Hooke, *Medieval Villages* (1985), pp.214-223

P. Rahtz and L. Watts, *Wharram Percy. The Memorial Stones of the Churchyard* (York University Archaeological Publications 1,1983)

A. Wager, 'Three centuries of death: a study of attitudes reflected in gravestones in Shenstone (Staffs) churchyard', *Transactions of the South Staffordshire Archaeological and Historical Society*, 19 (1979), pp.47-55

H. L. White, 'Monumental Inscriptions', *The Genealogists' Magazine*, 16 (1971), pp.470-474

E. G. Withycombe, 'Christian Names', *The Genealogists' Magazine*, 10, number 2 (1947), pp. 41-48

Dissertations:

J. C. Jones, 'The grave memorials of the church of St Mary, Deerhurst, Gloucestershire' (University of Birmingham, School of History, unpublished BA dissertation), 1972

L Pratt, 'A study of the grave memorials of the churches of Hillesden, Maids Moreton and Twyford (Bucks)', (University of Birmingham, School of History, unpublished BA dissertation), 1998

I. Shorters, 'A study of the grave memorials of Holy Trinity Church, Baswich, Staffordshire' (University of Birmingham, School of History, unpublished BA dissertation), 2000

www.ingramcontent.com/pod-product-compliance
Lightning Source LLC
Chambersburg PA
CBHW061304270326
41932CB00029B/3474